The Move to Mexico Bible

Sonia Diaz and Beverley Wood

ISBN 978-1-71-995291-0

First edition 2018
Eleventh revision 2025

Published by White Dog Publishing
info@whitedogcreative.com
www.whitedogcreative.com

Design/layout: Georgios Vasilopoulos
Zihuatanejo-Ixtapa photo: Meyrick Jones

Table of contents

Introduction

So, you're thinking about trying out Mexico? Good for you. I made the move in 2012—from the west coast of Canada with a husband and two dogs (and Sonia is from Mexico). There's a lot to discover about the process and a lot to remember as you go through it. It's exciting to plan your adventure and even more exciting to live it.

You've picked a great country. InterNations, a Munich-based network of 4.8 million expats, compiled survey statistics in 2024 of 12,500 expats worldwide—the average expat in Mexico is 56 years old and gender is split 51% male/49% female. Mexico ranked number two out of 53 countries for expats overall and took the top spot for happiness and finding friends. It ranked second for both ease of settling in and leisure options, as well as in culture. Mexico has consistently ranked in the top five since the first InterNations survey in 2014. No wonder more than half of expats say they plan to stay there forever.

And maybe you will too. But what you need is knowledge of local customs, laws and procedures to make your transition a smooth one. We hope we can help with that.

You will need to decide on a lot of things before you make the move. Like where you are going. Mexico is a big country and living in Tulum is nothing like living in Mexico City—and neither is anything like living in Puerto Vallarta. The food is different, the culture is different, the weather is different. It's an incredible country with many unique living experiences to choose from.

And there are other questions. What will you do for medical insurance? Will you be bringing your vehicle and pets? Are you allowed to own property in Mexico? How do you handle paying utilities?

Can you transfer money online easily? How long can you stay? Will you have to pay taxes? Do you have enough money to live there?

The Move to Mexico Bible takes a look at 33 cities and towns—from expat populations to climate and conveniences. This book will also walk you through the visa process and give you invaluable advice about healthcare, household help, communications, real estate and other variables. Don't leave home without it! While there will always many more questions to be answered—fear not. It's a painless process if you are prepared and understand what you need to do. It really is. And there's no time like now to start reading up.

As a note of caution—Mexico uses the metric system of weights and measures with temperatures in degrees Celsius (°C) and distances in kilometers (km), measurements in meters (m), weights in kilograms (kg) and so on. Canada also uses the metric system—so does everyone in the world except the USA, Liberia and Myanmar (and the UK for long distances). Out of courtesy to our readers from the US, we have included approximate—and I mean approximate—equivalents for you using the Imperial system.

We have also converted Mexican pesos to US dollars for the purposes of this book at MX$20 per US$1. Please be sure to check current exchange rates.

—Beverley Wood

Chapter 1:

The big move

The first question is, of course: Where in Mexico do you want to live? It's a big country.

There are three points to consider when choosing a region in Mexico—crime, climate and geography.

Crime in Mexico

Let's just get right to the elephant in the room. Should you be afraid to move to Mexico? More than a million expats here say no. That said, you need to be aware.

Because of the movement of drugs north from Latin American countries (and some domestically grown) to USA, there is crime in Mexico that can be quite hideous and violent. But almost without exception, it is related to cartels and/or drugs.

You need to prepare yourself. Especially if you are reading English-language newspapers based in Mexico, you are going to wake up some mornings to images of bodies swinging from bridges as the sun comes up and the commuter traffic begins. Or a dozen bodies lined up at the side of the highway, all bound and blindfolded, all dead. It happens and, believe me, this is cartel-related—and often not anywhere near where you are planning to settle.

Although there have been pretty grisly discoveries almost everywhere, it is most common in the border towns and the states with warring criminal elements. When cartels start to fight over territories, all hell breaks loose.

If this talk makes you nervous, you can follow the (very conservative and cautious) advice of the governments of Canada, USA and many other countries. They issue warnings regularly about which states are hot-spots for violence from cartels competing for territory. Then you can take these places off your potential list from the start. As you live in Mexico, you will gain more confidence. The cartel wars really will not affect the average person. I've been here seven years, incident-free.

In 2023, Mexico had an overall murder rate of 24 per 100,000. As a national average, that's high, but it's driven up by cities like Colima at 140, Tijuana at 84, and Ciudad Juárez at 68. Many tourist areas, however, remain relatively unaffected. For example, Puerto Vallarta, on the Pacific Coast, reported 15 homicides per 100,000—lower than Dallas TX, which had a rate of 19.

All this said, as long as you aren't traveling at night, you stay on the toll roads and busy highways, you are safe to drive through most states. I wouldn't meander much—but don't worry about driving through on your way to somewhere else during the daylight hours. And if you need to stop overnight, there are plenty of hotels surrounded by large walls.

Travelers in any country are targets for thieves. Don't wear fancy jewelry, don't get drunk and fall down on the sidewalk at 2am, and don't flash a lot of cash around. Be aware. As aware as you would be in any place that is foreign to you.

Climate and geography

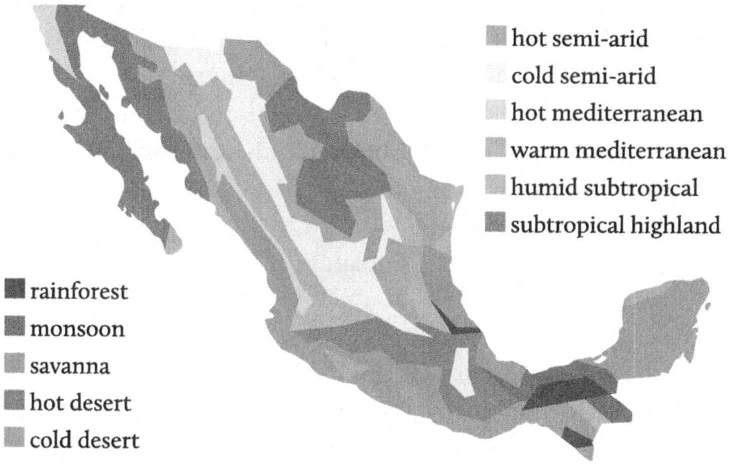

Climate and geography go hand-in-hand in one sense—your elevation, proximity to the coast and latitudinal location will all affect the climate. But another consideration of geography is proximity to the northern border for driving—or proximity to an international airport for easy plane rides to visit friends and family. It's possible you plan to move to Mexico and rarely leave, in which case those two considerations will be of limited value to you.

You'll make choices according to your personal situations. Being close to an airport may be of great importance or none at all. If you have respiratory problems, you may need to look at sea level locations only.

Mexico's topography runs from sea level to 5,636 m above sea level (18,491 ft). For comparison, Denver CO is 1,609 m (5,280 ft) above sea level. The highest point in Mexico is Pico de Orizaba near Puebla in the Trans-Mexican volcanic mountain belt. The air's pretty thin up there.

There are a good number of major cities in what is known as the central highlands that rest 1,500–2,000 m (5,000–6,500 ft) above sea level, such as Ajijic, San Miguel and Cuernavaca. And then there's Mexico City, the country's capital and 22nd largest city in the world (ahead of both London and New York but trailing cities like Tokyo and Shanghai).

Other charming cities in the highlands include Morelia, Pátzcuaro and San Luis Potosí.

The air in the highlands can be thin for some people—if you suffer from chronic obstructive pulmonary disease (COPD), for example, or if you are overweight. You may feel unusually tired for a few days after you arrive, possibly longer. But for most of us, you get used to the altitude in a matter of days.

There are big daily climate differences between the central highlands, the beaches and the north. The north, for example, gets snow (and a fair bit of it). Bet you didn't know that. Few of you will move there—the weather in Mexico is, after all, one of the biggest attractions—and we're not going to go there, anyway.

And, of course, the further south you get, the warmer the beaches—and the mountains—are. There is a lot of beach to choose from: Mexico has 9,330 km of coastline (5,779 mi).

We've included average monthly high and low temperature ranges and humidity averages in each region. Humidity is very important in judging the climate. If you can handle heat and humidity—the beach is your place. If not, the central or southern highlands provide a tropical climate mitigated by elevation and they are not as humid or hot. But parts can be very cool in the winter months at night.

The climate in and around Cuernavaca, for example, on the southern slope of Mexico City's Sierra Chichinautzin mountain, is very temperate. The city was dubbed *City of Eternal Spring* by Alexander von Humboldt. Nonetheless, it **can** reach upper single digits (°C) overnight (high-40s °F) during the coldest period, which generally falls mid-January to mid-February.

San Miguel de Allende, at slightly lower elevation, is further north and is considered a mid-latitude desert climate, reaching below freezing temperatures overnight on some January and February nights. You may even need to cover your plants from frost occasionally. And while it warms up during the day, sunny and often reaching 25–28°C midday (mid-80s °F), there is no such thing as central heating in Mexico.

Most of the houses are masonry (solid cement) and they will absorb the cold and hold it—as well as the heat in the summer. Forewarned is forearmed.

Mexico has seven different climate regions ranging from tropical to Mediterranean—spread out over 32 states, four oceans or seas, along with jungles, mountains and deserts. So, you have choices.

There are two tropical climates—wet and wet-dry. The first has at least 60 mm (2.4") of rain each and every month of the year. This climate is found in the Gulf Coastal Plain—southern Veracruz and Tabasco, also in the Oaxacan and Chiapan highlands to the south.

It is the tropical wet-dry climate that is found in much of coastal Mexico including the Pacific from Nayarit all the way to the southern border, as well as Cancún, central and northern Veracruz and the Yucatán Peninsula. The winter months get less than 40 mm (1.5") of rain while the summer months receive more than 150 mm (6").

The best news about these tropical climates is that the temperature does not normally dip below 18°C (65°F). It will get hot in the summer, however.

And, correspondingly, Mexico has two dry climates. Arid desert climates receive less than 250 mm (10") of rain all year. In Mexico, dry desert areas include western Sonora province in the north and most of Baja California as well as Ciudad Juárez at the border with El Paso TX.

The semi-arid desert areas receive 250–750 mm (10–30") of rain a year with a savanna climate. It includes most of the central plateau and western Sierra Madre, as well as other inland areas. Rains fall mostly in the summer and heavy thunderstorms are common.

There are three temperate zones—dry winter, humid subtropical and Mediterranean.

Temperate dry winter zones have mild temperatures, low humidity and rain in summertime (600–1,200 mm or 25–45" per year). It includes much of the central highlands as well as parts of Nuevo León and Tamaulipas in the north. The 'volcanic axis' sits squarely in this zone. Altitude controls the temperature and creates a mosaic of micro-climates.

The humid tropical zone is, as it says, humid and gets rain throughout the year. The Tropic of Cancer, at about 23.5° latitude, is what divides the country into temperate and tropical zones. Most of the country experiences the rainy season in the summer, from May–September. July is the wettest month, February is the driest.

A portion of northwestern Baja California, in the Ensenada area, experiences the last (and perhaps most desirable) climate—Mediterranean. You'll find lots of wineries and olive trees in this zone.

There are also hurricanes to contend with in beach locations, and earthquakes in both the mountains and some coastal areas. The risk you assign to this is really your own choice—we know some people who live on the beach who feel perfectly secure in their ability to survive a massive hit (and, indeed, they have already lived through a close call). We live in Cuernavaca but feel that because our house is situated on one mother of a volcanic rock shelf, earthquake damage is unlikely. But we all know that anything can happen. Mexico does have devastating hurricanes on both coasts and it is one of the most seismically active countries in the world. But it's also a big country geographically and some areas seem more susceptible than others. Choose your location wisely if you plan to make it your home (that goes for anywhere in the world).

We've collected some data about some of the most popular towns in each region to help you choose the places you'd like to research further and even visit—with an eye to moving to Mexico.

Chapter 2:

North Pacific coast

Mazatlán, Puerto Vallarta, Manzanillo

Obviously beach towns are at sea level. If you have problems with altitude, this is where you should be looking. If you have problems with heat and humidity part of the year, this is not where you should be looking. The beach towns have high humidity most of the year, peaking in the summer. That said, there is a lot of different geography to cover when you start to talk beach towns, and a lot of options, so don't rule out anywhere yet.

Mexico has more than 9,000 km (5,600 mi) of coastline on three different bodies of water—technically four, but I can't count the

Caribbean Sea with the same weight, as it's a very small portion of Mexican geography. The country runs 3,200 km (2,000 mi) from Tijuana in the north west to Cancún in the south east.

Cuisine is seafood-based on Mexico's coastlines—lots of aguachile (ceviche), seafood soups and stews.

One thing to note, true of all beach towns, if you plan on living right on the beach—salt rusts everything. You will not be able to keep items made of any kind of metal—if they are mandatory, be prepared to replace them annually.

We'll talk about some of the most populous—and popular—spots, beginning with the beach towns on the Pacific Ocean, then moving to Baja California and the Gulf Coast.

Mazatlán

Founded in 1531 and known as the *The Pearl of the Pacific*, Mazatlán sits on Mexico's Pacific coast, across the Sea of Cortés from the tip of the Baja Peninsula. It just makes the cut—if you look north from town, you are not looking at the Pacific Ocean at all, but at the Sea of Cortés. In fact, there is an overnight ferry that travels from Mazatlán to La Paz on the Baja Peninsula.

Mazatlán has great winter weather—around 28°C and is sunny, sunny, sunny. Temperatures in the higher 30s °C (90+°F) come alongside high humidity in the summer. July, August and September are the height of the rainy season, although it can sometimes arrive earlier or remain later. Some people who live at the beach are able to leave during the hottest summer months. Others hunker down with air conditioning, at movie theaters or in the pool.

There are other factors to consider besides climate (and the winter weather is awesome). Mazatlán has many of the conveniences of home and is a substantial city where expats feel welcome. While learning Spanish is always recommended, you can get by here speaking only English.

Mazatlán has an international airport (MZT), although direct flights are limited. Currently, there are direct flights from the west coast of Canada and the USA and assorted domestic destinations—check online for more information.

The city boasts more than 485,000 residents and has a charming, colonial-era historic center with shops, restaurants and boutiques housed in restored buildings.

The Zona Dorada (Golden Zone), along 6 km (4 mi) of pristine beaches, is primarily hotels and condominiums (and nightlife at the hotel bars). Many expats buy here and enjoy stunning sunset views over the Pacific.

At the north end of the city, near the new convention center (the largest in Mexico), there are upscale residential developments being built alongside the only PGA golf course on the Pacific.

You'll find Walmart, Home Depot and Sam's Club as well as a plethora of great supermarkets. There are organic markets, farmers' markets and a large central public market where Mexicans begin selling their fresh fruit, vegetables, meats, poultry in the early morning.

In Mazatlán, the public hospitals include IMSS Hospital General and the ISSSTE Clinica Hospital. Two of the private hospitals with good reputations include Sharp Hospital and Marina Mazatlán, but there are many more. Check local directories for your options.

In summary, Mazatlán is a decent-sized city with convenient shopping, an expat population, beaches and sunshine. Do remember, it can be hot and muggy in the summer and the airport isn't the best in the off-season. You need to come down here in the summer and get a feel for the climate and the accessibility. Some people love the off-season when the tourists go home. Others hightail it north to visit family, or into the mountains to beat the heat.

Puerto Vallarta

Officially founded in 1851, this quaint fishing village on the Pacific Coast exploded with tourist activity in the 1960s, thanks to John Huston's *The Night of the Iguana* being set there—starring Ava Gardner and Richard Burton. Situated on the Pacific Coast at the Bay of Banderas, it lies 450 km (280 mi) south of Mazatlán.

The rainy season runs June to September and these are marvelous tropical rains. Of course, they also come with the hurricane season—not insignificant—that runs from mid-May until mid-October. During the summer months the daytime high temperatures run over 30°C (90°F). The humidity is higher in the rainy season but rarely falls below 70%. During the winter, the weather is perfect with highs in the upper-20s °C (80s °F) and lows of 18–20°C (70°F).

There is a large expat community in Puerto Vallarta and many social events organized by the various groups. It's easy to speak only English here if you stick to the gringo haunts and don't assimilate much. And most stores and restaurants have staff that all speak English—this is tourist town first and foremost with tourism constituting over 50% of the town's economy.

There is a large LGBT tourist community and the town holds a gay pride parade annually over the US Memorial Day weekend. When you throw in the numerous cruise ships stopping in the bay, it's easy to see why Puerto Vallarta has been dubbed the *San Francisco of Mexico*.

The international airport (PVR) is busy—it handles almost 7 million passengers a year, with 73% of those passengers being international. However, Puerto Vallarta also remains a popular domestic vacation spot, with Mexican tourist traffic peaking on holiday weeks such as Christmas and Semana Santa (Easter). Major US, Mexican and Canadian airlines all fly here, with increased frequency during winter months. Major Canadian cities have direct fights.

The municipal population is nearing 500,000 and it's the second largest city in Jalisco state (behind Guadalajara). It's hard to estimate how many gringos live in Puerto Vallarta, but certainly tens of thousands. And during the winter months, the international airport processes 700,000 tourists per month.

Many expats live on the hill above Old Town, a neighborhood that's aptly named Gringo Gulch. Dotted with low-rise condos, their views of the Pacific are spectacular. Old Town is in the center of the city, with its charming shops, seafood bars and colonial architecture. And Puerto Vallarta boasts an awesome malecón (walkway) by the ocean with stunning Mexican art on permanent display.

The beaches of Puerto Vallarta, north and south, are expansive and they are swimming beaches (which is not true of all locations on the Pacific Coast).

Nuevo Vallarta is just 10 minutes north of the airport and is actually located in Nayarit state, although, for many, it is a Puerto Vallarta suburb. It was a government project 20 years ago that now contains marinas, condominiums, luxury villas and estates.

South out of Puerto Vallarta is where you'll find the stunning architectural homes perched out over the cliffs, sitting on the edge of the jungle. There are several colonias (neighborhoods) that expats are drawn to including El Centro, the Romantic Zone (Old Town), 5 de Deciembre, Marina Vallarta, and Fluvial Vallarta in the north.

You'll find all the big box stores—Walmart, Costco, Sam's Club et al, many supermarkets, and public and farmers' markets. In addition, being a tourist town, there are many traditional Mexican artisan creations—colorful hammocks and poncho blankets, Huichol Indian pieces, Talavera pottery and so much more. Many of the larger, more commercial stores tend to be in the north of town and folk art outlets and markets can be found in Old Town.

In Puerto Vallarta, the public hospitals include the Regional Hospital Puerto Vallarta and the IMSS Clinic. The private hospitals are very well-respected—PV is a medical tourism destination. Private facilities include the Vallarta Medical Center, Hospiten Puerto Vallarta and Hospital San Javier Marina.

In summary, the town is a bit touristy but it's large enough and diverse enough to be interesting on a year-round basis. That is, if you can either handle the humidity in the summer, or go somewhere to escape the season. Although, our view is that since you're picking your place to live, you shouldn't have to be thinking about escaping for a season already. If Puerto Vallarta is in your sights, we really encourage you to spend some time there in the rainy (and muggy) season because you already know the winter is perfect.

Manzanillo

Manzanillo is the busiest port city in all of Mexico, receiving all ocean cargo destined for Mexico City. Discovered in the 1500s by the Spanish, it was an important port for them and for 300

years became the target of international pirates. A tourist destination, the city has spectacular beaches and many self-contained resorts for tourists who may be nervous of crime—one of which is the famous Las Hadas (The Fairies) where the movie *10* was shot, starring Bo Derek and Dudley Moore. It's also known as the *Sailfish Capital of Mexico* and has a vibrant sport fishing industry. It's not a big gringo city and, aside from the beach-front properties, is quite industrial and Mexican-looking.

High temperatures almost always hit 30+°C (90+°F), no matter what time of year, and the rainy season is May–July. While the humidity will dip to around 60% in the winter, most of the rainy season is almost 100% humidity. The rainy season in Manzanillo is hot, oppressive and overcast. January, February and March have fantastic weather with sunny days and nighttime temperatures dipping to 18°C (70°F).

In the tourist resort areas, you'll find more people who speak English. But this is a port city first and a tourist city second—the town center will find you mingling with Mexican locals as they go about their daily routines. If you plan to assimilate and can learn a little Spanish, living here is not a problem. But you shouldn't count on getting by on English alone.

The Manzanillo airport (ZLO) is international, but small, and many cities in the US and Canada will only have direct flights in the busy winter months. The airport is located about 35 km north of the city and estimated to handle about 250,000 tourists in the winter months.

The population of Manzanillo is getting close to 200,000—so it's a city, not a town. And, with the exception of the resort and beach areas north of town, it's an industrial city. And very Mexican. Huge cranes define the skyline in the older part of the city at the port. Other beach towns we've talked about have more tourism and more expat residents. The gringo money drives those towns. This is a Mexican working city by contrast.

Las Brisas, the area south of the city plaza, was the original beach-front where all the hotels were built. The older hotels are showing their age but the area is still quaint and home to some gringos. The more popular neighborhood is the Santiago area in the north of town. It has a smaller town feel and great beaches (waves in the Las Brisas beach area can be very rough). Santiago isn't touristy, but full of mercados (markets) and places to buy fresh fruit and fresh-off-the-boat fish. There are gated communities if that is your preference. The Juluapan Peninsula, a little further north of Santiago, is starting to see a gringo influx. It's a little further out but has killer views and affordable property.

Manzanillo has the major supermarkets—Soriana and Comercial Mexicana (La Comer et al). There is also a large Walmart store and a Sam's Club, Office Max, Burger King, KFC—enough American franchises to make you wish they'd stop now. They have added a Home Depot in recent years, but no Costco yet.

To be frank, we find Sam's Club and Walmart lacking here in Mexico—even the Walmart Súper stores have sub-par (for Mexico) produce and poor-quality household goods from China. But there is always superb online shopping at Amazon Mexico and MercadoLibre for household goods—see *Online shopping (in your pajamas)* in *Chapter 24: Handy guides* for a list.

The public hospitals in Manzanillo include Hospital General de Manzanillo and Hospital IMSS. Private options include Hospital Médica Pacifico and Hospital Manzanillo.

Overall, there's a lot to offer in Manzanillo if you want to live in a real working Mexican city (albeit small city) and can take the summer heat. Plenty of conveniences, but you don't have the 'tourist pretty' that you do in places like Puerto Vallarta's Old Town, San Miguel's Centro or the malecón at Lake Chapala. Still, you get a more authentic Mexico. This town might have been on our list, if it weren't for the climate. The hot and humid is a non-starter in our world but Manzanillo is worth checking out if want to live on the beach. Just be sure to check it out in the summer.

Chapter 3:

South Pacific coast

Zihuatanejo-Ixtapa, Acapulco, Puerto Escondido

We're getting further south, so it's going to be even more hot and humid in the winter. But we're further away from the masses, too—which is a plus. And we're on the ocean.

Warm water fish like mahi-mahi, tuna, shrimp and red snapper are plentiful in the coastal cuisine. And as you get further south, more meat-based and Mayan cuisine choices become available, as the south of Mexico has a large indigenous population.

Zihuatanejo-Ixtapa

South of Manzanillo just 440 km (250 mi), you'll find the oceanfront towns of Zihuatanejo and Ixtapa. Just 5 km (3 mi) from each other, the two towns couldn't be any different. Ixtapa was a government tourism creation in the early 1970s. Zihuatanejo was a sleepy fishing village surrounded by haciendas. It was purposely developed for tourism at the same time as the creation of Ixtapa but still retains its Mexican charm. Settled by the Spaniards in the 1500s, it has colonial architecture and old-world charm. It's the third most visited area in Mexico, after Cancún and Puerto Vallarta.

Year-round highs are 30+°C—we're on the beach and we're going further south. The rainy season is June to September and humidity runs 70–80% year-round, with the most humid month being September.

In the tourist areas, particularly in Zihuatanejo compared to Ixtapa, most people speak English. Tourism is the reason this area exists and most of the tourists speak English. If you're going to live in the area, it would be wise to learn some Spanish in order to be able to venture away from the tourist locations.

Ixtapa-Zihuatanejo International Airport (ZIH) handles 650,000 passengers a year and has direct flights from major cities. These flights are reduced or eliminated in the off-season, but it's easy to get to Mexico City and take a domestic flight from there.

The population of the municipality is estimated to be 13,000. Proportionately, few are gringos but there are gringos in town (and on the beach). They tend to mix both with other gringos and nationals.

The seaside city's biggest asset are its beaches—well-sheltered from the Pacific Ocean. It's what made the area the third most popular tourist destination in Mexico. Playa La Madera, Playa La Ropa and El Hujal are where many foreigners choose to live in town. The areas are close to the beach, shopping and entertainment, and check most gringo boxes.

Aside from tourism, fishing continues to be a way of life and fresh catches of tuna, marlin and grouper can be bought right off the docks. There are large supermarkets, the ubiquitous farmers' markets or mercados and also a Sam's Club.

There are good private and public hospitals in Zihuatanejo/Ixtapa including Hospital General de Zihuatanejo/IMSS Hospital (public) and Clinica Mediciel (private), among others. Sanatorio Naval has a hyperbaric chamber—important information for divers.

In summary, more of a Mexican fishing town atmosphere on the Zihuatanejo side and smaller overall than other cities we've discussed, so somewhat fewer amenities—no Costco or Home Depot, for example. It's also quite hot, especially in September, so you need to visit then to ensure that the humidity won't make it unbearable for you. Of course, there's always the option of planning to visit friends and family in the hottest months—you need to make choices that work for you.

Acapulco

With its deep, circular bay—Acapulco de Juárez has been a port city since the early colonial times in Mexico and still serves as a cruise ship and commercial shipping port. Acapulco came into her own as a resort town during the 1940–60s. The 1963 Elvis film *Fun in Acapulco* really put this resort town on the US vacation map. That, and it being frequented by such Hollywood stars as Frank Sinatra and Elizabeth Taylor. It was *the* place to go.

Acapulco is Mexico's largest beach and spa resort city—with the caveat that most tourism to Acapulco these days is from within Mexico. This is due to the violence that has fallen upon the city due to an influx in cartel activity and, to a certain extent, the way those activities are covered by the media outside of Mexico. It has been violent, no question. And international tourism has decreased by 85% in the last decade. It is included in this book because of its history and beauty but many consider this city to be yesterday's news. It was enjoying a bit of a comeback with well-heeled domestic tourists, but Hurricane Otis in 2023 and subsequent storms have damaged the infrastructure in some areas.

Located on the Pacific coast, just under 400 km (240 mi) from Mexico City, Acapulco enjoys a stable climate year-round. Average highs are in the low-30s °C (90+°F) and it dips slightly below 20°C (72°F) at night some months. It has a very distinct wet season from June through October. However, the humidity also remains steady year-round at about 75%.

While English used to be more common in tourist areas, you may find that changing, as the tourists are now predominantly Mexican. If you choose to live in Acapulco, you will want to learn some Spanish.

Acapulco International Airport (ACA) handles around 700,000 passengers a year and has direct flights year-round from major US and Canadian cities. It's a four-hour drive from Mexico City along the new toll road, making it a convenient getaway for Chilangos (residents of Mexico City).

The population of Acapulco has dropped to 650,000, but it is still a major Mexican city and the largest in Guerrero state. One recent trending neighborhood, and a good choice for a residence, is Zona Diamante on the south side of the bay, across from Old Acapulco. With stunning beaches, major hotels and upscale amenities, this is where well-to-do Mexicans vacation and many local gringos have settled.

From open air markets to high-end (and I mean high-end) shopping malls, from tacky souvenirs to Cartier pearls, Acapulco is one of the top resort shopping destinations in Mexico. With almost three-quarters of a million people, it has every store you need (Costco, Home Depot, Office Depot et al), a multitude of fresh produce and seafood and, if you want, super high-end shopping.

Public hospitals include Hospital General Acapulco and Hospital IMSS Hospital General Regional Vicente Guerrero. There are many good private hospitals, as there are many wealthy residents.

Hospital Papagayo and Hospital y Torre Médica Santa Lucía have stellar reputations, but check local directories for more options.

Acapulco has a lot going for it and we do hear of gringos moving into Zona Diamante and living quite happily. It's worth checking out if the climate—and atmosphere—appeals to your taste. Stay in a reputable hotel and take their advice on the areas to avoid and those to embrace. There is still a lot of cartel conflict in the area—crime is still increasing in Acapulco, so do your research if this your choice.

Puerto Escondido (with a nod to Huatulco), Oaxaca

Puerto Escondido and Bahías de Huatulco are two very different destinations. Puerto Escondido (hidden port) was founded in 1928 as a small port to ship coffee, along with a bit of fishing. Huatulco was developed as a tourist destination in the 1980s (much like Cancún). Huatulco is more a collection of satellite beach locations with five-star hotels, made up of nine bays, including the popular cruise ship port of call in Santa Cruz Bay.

Puerto Escondido is a much more laid-back destination with surfers, hippies, cafés and bistros. It was just a small fishing village that occasionally acted as a port, but had no potable water until the mid-20th century. In the 1960s, Highway 200 connected the Oaxacan coastal towns with Acapulco—and Puerto Escondido became the largest tourist draw in Oaxaca state. It is 400 km from Acapulco and almost twice that from Mexico City. Flight time from Mexico City is just one hour.

Puerto is a big enough town to retain its own 'vibe' and not turn into the kind of tourist destination that comes out of a glossy magazine. It's still a Mexican town with fishermen, vendors and local culture. Hard to say that about its counterpart, Huatulco, which does, admittedly, have better swimming beaches but is a recently-manufactured resort area. Physically the two towns are about 100 km (60 mi) apart and share the same climates.

And the climate here is tropical—make no mistake. It's also pretty consistent. Highs in the upper-20s °C (88°F) most months, with the hotter months, around May, reaching into the 30s °C (90s °F).

It rains the most in May and June and it can be torrential. Rainy season runs from May to October and humidity runs 75% all year.

Being a real Mexican working town (despite also being a hippie town), it's helpful to know Spanish. In any tourist-related venues, they will speak English, but if you're planning to live here, you'll want to know some Spanish.

Now, here's the bad news—the airport is primarily used as a domestic airport. But the good news is, you can get to Mexico City multiple times a day in about an hour, and you can fly direct to anywhere from there. Puerto Escondido International Airport (PXM) handles about 250,000 passengers a year.

The population is about 50,000 and, as noted, it does have a small gringo community. It's getting large enough to have some services but if you're looking for Costco or Walmart you're out of luck. However, the Benito Juárez market is open every day and, while fairly typical of Mexican markets, is better laid out than most. The town has a Chedraui, an upscale supermercado (supermarket), but box stores are few and far between.

In Puerto Escondido there is public Hospital General Puerto Escondido. Note that if you are in Huatulco, Hospital General San Pedro is closer. There are good private hospitals including Hospital Ángel del Mar (Puerto Escondido) and Grupo Medico Huatulco.

In summary, this is a very authentic, affordable town with a laid-back and eccentric population of gringos among the locals. Good internet service is available but parts of town are slow, so be sure to do speed check tests before making any commitments if it's important to you. If I wanted to be on the beach, in this kind of climate, this would be my kind of town.

Chapter 4:

Baja California and Baja California Sur

Ensenada, La Paz, Todos Santos, Los Cabos

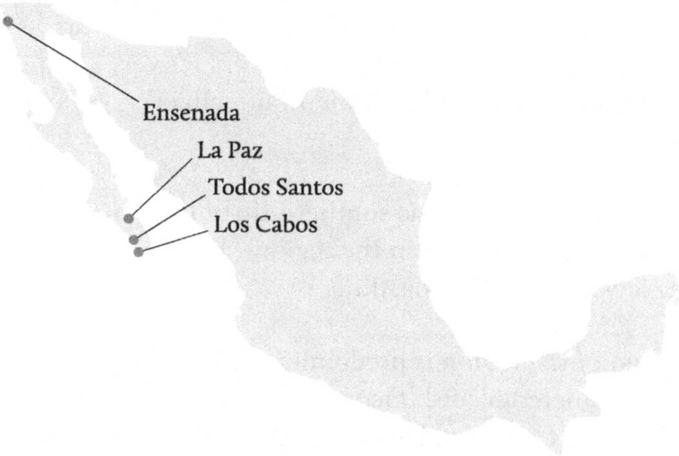

The Mexican states of Baja California and Baja California Sur confuse some. While the name *Las Californias* (for both Mexico and the USA) originated with the Spaniards in the 16th century when they came to the Americas, it has nothing to do with the US state of California, other than currently sharing a border.

The Baja Peninsula runs from the northern border town of Tijuana to the southern town of Cabo San Lucas, sitting between the Pacific Ocean and the Gulf of California. South of Mexicali, the peninsula separates from mainland Mexico around the Gulf of California (also known as the Sea of Cortés). There is a ferry service from La Paz, on the Gulf of California, to Mazatlán, Sinaloa. It is an overnight ferry service and takes about seven hours to cross.

Listen up, this is important—the states of Baja California and Baja California Sur have an advantage when it comes to bringing a foreign car into the country. There is no import duty and no temporary import sticker (TIP) required. So, you can drive your foreign-plated car, as long as you keep the original registration and plates current. You do need to purchase Mexican insurance, but you can even do that online.

This is a big bonus for expats who want to keep their cars, as you'll see in the transportation section later on. It's very complicated to bring your car in, and it's time-limited in every other part of the country.

Cabo (as it's called), on the southern tip of the peninsula, is the best-known beach town in the region—but there are plenty of other jewels along the coastline.

The food of the region is predominated by seafood—of course. You'll find incredible fish tacos everywhere you go. Cabo is the center of the farm-to-table movement and the emphasis in the peninsula is on wine, olives and olive oil. Baja-Med, as they call it.

Ensenada, Baja California

Ensenada is a mere 125 km (80 mi) south of San Diego on the Pacific Ocean. Locally referred to *La Bella Cenicienta del Pacífico* (the beautiful Cinderella of the Pacific), the city was founded by the Spaniards in 1542. It gained popularity during US prohibition as an entertainment and drinking spot, and subsequently developed as a tourist town. It is the jumping-off point for Valle de Guadalupe, the Napa Valley of Mexico.

The economic focus of the town is tourism and technology, and it is growing as a scientific and biotech research center. There are plans for rail transport between Ensenada and San Diego, and there has been a huge influx of biotech companies in the past few years.

It's also a cruise ship port, and home to the Baja 1000 and Baja 500 off-road races held every November and June, respectively.

As a mild, semi-arid climate, winter temperatures range from 10–20°C (50–70°F) and summer temps from 15–25°C (60–80°F). You will, on a cold year, get single digits Celsius (mid-40s °F) on a few nights. But it is one of the most moderate climates in all of Mexico—grapes and olives thrive here. In fact, Mexico's wine-growing region—Valle de Guadalupe—is only 20 km (12 mi) from Ensenada. *The Independent* in the UK called it 'the best wine-making region you have never heard of'.

The rainy period runs December through March and on occasion can bring heavy rain. And it's on the ocean, so there is constant humidity (in the 65–75% range on average) but the temperatures are much more moderate than beach towns further south, so it is far less oppressive.

While speaking Spanish is helpful, you can get by without it here. There is a large gringo community, including some Canadians and Europeans, but many more Americans due to the driving proximity. You should learn some Spanish anyway—you'll get a lot more out of the city, as it is the first language for many of the residents.

Unfortunately, the closest international airport is in Tijuana (TIJ), just over an hour to the north. There are direct flights to US locations but you can't get to Canada or Europe without stopping in Mexico City. There is a small airport in Ensenada (ESE) which may see commercial flights in future as tourism increases.

You may also fly into San Diego (SAN), just north of the border and take a bus. The real advantage here is for those who wish to travel by car—just 1.5 hours from the US border. And it's a great view drive along the ocean.

The population is about 500,000, making it a decent-sized city. Certainly, it is large enough to find all of the services you might ever want. Being close to the US border is considered a major plus, so housing is not as inexpensive as it can be in other parts of Mexico. Expats do settle all over town, but two popular areas are Baja Mar to the north and Punta Banda to the south.

The town has all the typical Mexican markets, supermarkets and department stores, as well as American box stores such as Costco, Walmart, Sam's Club and Home Depot. Nothing lacking in the shopping department—and San Diego is less than a two-hour drive if you do feel something is missing.

There are the standard public hospitals in Ensenada, including General Hospital and IMSS Clinic 8. In addition, there are many good private hospitals including Hospital Velmar, San Fernando Clinic and Cardiomed.

Although it might feel a little like you're only wetting your toes and you aren't really experiencing authentic Mexico, Ensenada can be the perfect place to live for lots of people. The climate is one of the best in all of Mexico and the most moderate. The proximity to the US is a plus for Americans. All the conveniences are available and, with a decent expat population, there is a lot of support in English as you learn the language and culture of your new country.

However, there has been an increase in homicides in the cities closest to the border since 2018, including Ensenada. While generally not tourist or expat-related, you still need to take appropriate precautions.

La Paz, Baja California Sur

La Paz was first inhabited more than 10,000 years ago by Neolithic hunter-gatherers but that's probably not relevant (interesting, though). In 1535 Cortés arrived, but left, and it wasn't until 1596 that the city was actually established. Because of its proximity to USA, it became a tourist destination in the 1970s when the Transpeninsular Highway from the USA/Mexico border was paved. It's a 1,500-km (930-mi) drive and takes approximately 18 hours. In addition, Baja Ferries runs an automobile ferry from La Paz to Mazatlán and back. There are two truck ferries (cars welcome) that run from La Paz operated by TMC (Transportación Marítima de California). One goes to Mazatlán, the other to Topolobampo (further north). In both cases, check schedules for days of operation. It's about a three-hour drive from Cabo San Lucas.

It's not, however, your typical tourist city and not really an international tourist destination yet, but does have one of the highest standards of living in Mexico. It's a commercial center and the municipality boasts 300,000 residents. It's very spread out—in geographic size, it is the fourth-largest municipality in all of Mexico. The main industries are silver mining, agriculture, fishing and pearl diving (yes, that's right) with ecotourism growing by leaps and bounds.

John Steinbeck visited in 1940 and described La Paz in his 1947 novel *The Pearl*. It must have made an impression on him—he also refers to it often in his 1951 travelogue *The Log from the Sea of Cortés*. La Paz also has its own Carnaval (Mardi Gras) the week before Lent.

The climate is fairly warm—registering over 30°C (90°F) most days from April to October, and humidity usually tops 60%. That said, rainfall is actually quite scant most of the year but the region sees heavy downpours in August and September. And, according to locals, being on the edge of the desert, it only feels humid from June through September. It does have more than 300 days of sunshine annually—for sun worshipers, this is a definite option.

The Isla Espíritu Santo group of islands off the Bay of La Paz in the Sea of Cortés has been designated as part of a larger UNESCO Biosphere Reserve and provides some of the best diving in Mexico. Great kayaking and snorkeling, too. The three leading marine biology institutes in Latin America call La Paz home.

All of Mexico has experienced a surge in crime in the past years, as previously noted. But as long as you adhere to common sense guidelines, there really is no danger. We will say it again in case you forgot. Don't walk around dark back alleys, while sober or drunk, at 2am. Don't flash a lot of cash or wear the Hope Diamond to dinner. It's just not done down here.

You'll need to speak some Spanish—many laborers and service people do not speak English. English is spoken at the beach and in stores, but not in local Mexican markets.

Manuel Márquez de León International Airport (LAP) handles 1.2 million passengers a year, and American Eagle offers direct flights to Phoenix and Dallas/Fort Worth. Mexican airline Volaris offers flights from La Paz to destinations in the USA through Mexico City as well as domestic flights. Please check their website.

Some of the best views in La Paz (and the most expensive properties) can be found in the neighborhoods of Pedregal de La Paz, Palmira and Costa Baja. Downtown also has a great deal to offer from waterfront condos to small houses. It's pedestrianized downtown and close proximity to the water means it's always in high demand.

Outside the city, the El Centenario neighborhood provides rural settings with views of the Sea of Cortés (a number of expats live in this area). And the gringos in La Paz are organized—so you'll find lots of gringo activities if that's what you're after, especially in the winter when the snowbirds return.

There's a great farmers' market on Tuesdays and Saturdays and, of course, the ubiquitous Sam's Club, City Club and Walmart, as well as the public markets. No Costco yet. But you should be able to find most of what you need—it's close enough to the border.

Public hospitals include Hospital General Juan María de Salvatierra, Hospital General Naval De La Paz and ISSSTE. Private hospitals include Medica Fidepaz, a favorite among expats.

In summary, this is a highly livable city if you can tolerate the summer heat. With a growing ecotourism sector, there is promise for future development and plenty of opportunity. You'll find most conveniences available (and you are close enough to the border) but remember, this is primarily a Mexican working city with an influx of snowbirds in the winter (many from California). You'll need at least some Spanish to survive.

Todos Santos, Baja California Sur

Founded as a Jesuit mission outpost in the early 1723, Todos Santos had very little future until the government paved Highway 19 from Cabo San Lucas, making it easily accessible to tourists.

It's a surfer town and artist community in the foothills of the Sierra de la Laguna mountains. It's located about 1,600 km (1,000 mi) south of San Diego and 75 km (45 mi) north of Cabo San Lucas. It sits quite close to the Tropic of Cancer.

It's a surfer town because there are great waves—which renders most of the beaches unsuitable for swimming (there are swimming beaches within a short drive).

The main industries are agriculture (mangoes, chiles, avocados, papayas and vegetables), tourism and fishing. There have been some major developments in the beach-front condo sector and some large money has landed in the area. The town itself is probably best known for the hotel/bar and gift shop known as Hotel California. After years of alluding to an *Eagles* connection, the band successfully sued the company for implying they were in any way related and the hotel settled the suit in early 2018.

The coldest months are December and January, with average highs of 25°C (77°F) and lows of 12°C (50°F). July through October is the 30+°C weather (90+°F) but note the plus sign. It can go much higher and humidity is almost always 80% or higher throughout the entire year (you're on water). There are ocean breezes—but it's warm in the summer. The rainy season is mid-July to mid-October, with September being the wettest month.

You can get by on the main strip—the tourist area—without speaking any Spanish. But in town, and to communicate with service people, you will likely have to speak some Spanish. Most of the expat community here stays away from the main drag and does make an effort to assimilate. It's a cute little spot that reminded me of a cross between a hippie and a hipster town (we almost bought a B&B there some years ago).

Los Cabos International Airport (SJD) is 60 km (40 mi) away and your best bet for international flights. It's the sixth-busiest airport in all of Mexico, handling almost 8 million passengers a year. There are many direct flights from US and Canadian cities during the winter months and a good number in the summer (but obviously fewer).

The airport at La Paz (LAP) is 70 km away (45 mi) and has many domestic and international flights (check Volaris). But it's a smaller airport. Check schedules to see which airport is more convenient.

The year-round population of Todos Santos is about 8,000. I meant it when I said small. Forget the box stores—but easy enough to head to either La Paz or Cabo San Lucas, where you'll find all the stores and more.

This is a small town and you'll be heading south to Cabo or north to La Paz for any major illness—but it's really not very far. There is a small medical center where you may be comfortable having most smaller procedures taken care of.

If you like small town living and can take the humidity, this could be your new home. It's an eclectic little town with a mix of the old and the new—but the new is clearly trendy and hip. The town is getting gentrified, and this could well become *the* spot on the cape in the future—making it a good investment today.

Los Cabos

Cabo San Lucas and San José del Cabo, Baja California Sur

Los Cabos (The Capes), as the municipality is known, consists of two very different towns, separated by a 32-km (20-mi) beach resort corridor full of high-end condominiums, hotels and golf courses. It was a remote and rural desert area until the government invested heavily in tourism in the 1970s. It was first discovered by the Spanish in the 16th century and many of the indigenous people were wiped out by European disease. For the most part, it remained an area isolated from the mainland until the tourism push began with Cabo San Lucas in 1974.

And, in fact, the city of Cabo San Lucas is so tourism-oriented that it doesn't have a plaza or main square, but focuses on the marina and entertainment areas. Make no mistake, this is tourist Mexico. But high-end tourist Mexico. George Clooney and Jennifer Aniston each have houses here and Sammy Hagar has made his Cabo Wabo tequila a household name. There is a decent expat population—and they have money. In fact, I offer a *Ruth's Chris Steak House* as irrefutable evidence.

However, off the beaten path, there is still an actual town behind the facade that can be quite charming. When the tourist upgrade arrived, it was a little fishing village, and the Mexican portion of the town is quite authentic still.

At the east end of the hotel corridor, San José del Cabo remains more of a real Mexican town—with a town square built around a 1700s church, cobblestone streets and colorful artisan shops. A few blocks in from the main square, despite the gentrification of the center of town, you'll find a real Mexican local market and inexpensive houses. It is the state capital and home to many upscale galleries, boutiques and restaurants.

Most of Baja California Sur is more expensive than other regions of Mexico. Partly the tourists, sure, but primarily the distance that products have to travel. It's a desert. It doesn't grow much. But it sits where the desert meets the sea and the Gulf of California meets the Pacific—and the climate can be spectacular. It is one of the sunniest locations in the world with an average of 320 sunny days a year.

There are lovely temperatures November–April, average highs of 25°C (80°F) and lows of 15°C (60°F). The warmer months, May–October, can be a challenge for some, with temperatures reaching the mid-30s °C most days (upper-90s °F). Rainy season runs July to October and the humidity is high then, up to 99% in

August and September but moderate during the winter months (desert, remember). But there's lots of air conditioning in this part of Mexico for the few humid months. And for clientele who don't need to watch their power consumption.

This is another one of those created Mexican tourist areas, so you never have to learn any Spanish if you don't want to. There is a large enough gringo population that you can find everything you need in English.

Los Cabos International Airport (SJD) is the sixth-busiest airport in all of Mexico, handling 5 million passengers a year. There are many direct flights from US and Canadian cities during the winter months and a good number in the summer (but obviously fewer).

The population of the municipality of Los Cabos is about 350,000—big enough to offer all of the services you might need, including Costco, Sam's Club and Walmart.

Cabo San Lucas itself is pretty Americanized, while the hotel corridor is very international and could be on any very good beach, anywhere in the world. Still, if you venture out of town, you can find some cool places—great farm-to-table restaurants and people doing pretty funky environmental things.

You could live anywhere in the municipality—but if I were looking for a Mexican experience, I would go find a charming old Mexican house off the beaten path in San José del Cabo. But, that said, plenty of people want to retire in luxury—in that case, head for the estates with some of the best views in the world in Pedregal Hills, on the Pacific side of Cabo San Lucas.

The standard public hospitals are available here, including Hospital General and Hospiten Cabo San Lucas. Given the number of very wealthy expats and snowbirds, private care is superb, and the town is also a major medical tourism destination. Some of the favored private facilities include AMC (American Medical Center) and Saint Luke's Hospitals.

All in all, a very comfortable place for well-to-do gringos to retire, and lots of opportunity for tourism businesses. About 2 million tourists hit these beaches every year and they've all got money to spend. You'd be wise to get out of town for August and September when temperatures reach the mid-30s °C (high-90s °F) and humidity runs 99%. There is also the strongest chance of hurricanes during these two months. Overall, not authentic Mexican unless you head a bit past the hotel zone, but one of the easiest places to live in Mexico. But not the most economical.

Chapter 5:

Gulf Coast and Riviera Maya

Veracruz, Campeche, Mérida, Cancún, Playa del Carmen, Akumal and Tulum

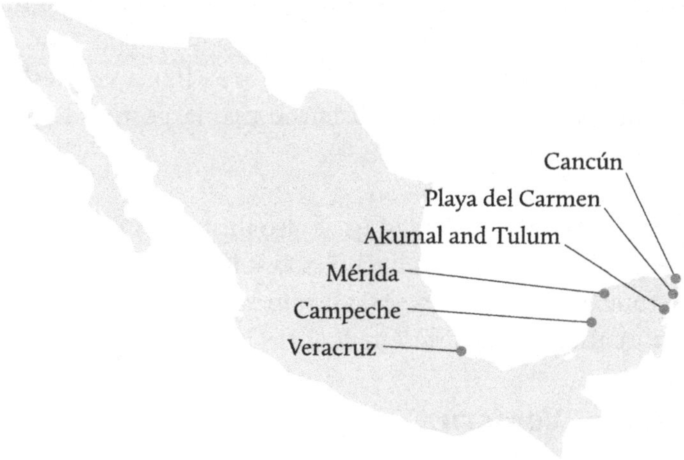

The Gulf of Mexico lies along the Mexican states of Tamaulipas, Veracruz, Tabasco, Campeche, Yucatán and the northern tip of Quintana Roo. The coastline is just under 3,000 km (1,900 mi).

The Gulf Coast, and especially Veracruz, has an Afro-Caribbean influenced cuisine—with spicy chile sauces and sweet tropical fruit, as well as vanilla which originated here.

At Cancún, the Gulf of Mexico meets the Caribbean Sea. And just south of Cancún, the Riviera Maya begins. It used to simply be called the Cancún–Tulum corridor, stretching from Playa del Carmen to Tulum, but the tourism department got creative.

The cuisine of the Yucatán is different from anywhere else in Mexico. It has a strong Mayan culinary tradition, as well as Caribbean, French and Middle Eastern influences. The spice achiote (annatto) is widely used, giving foods a reddish color. Many tropical fruits are utilized in cooking, such as tamarind, mamey and bitter oranges.

The Riviera Maya is completely within the state of Quintana Roo on the Yucatán Peninsula and is tropical. The region also has no surface rivers. However, the area has a very efficient subterranean system that boasts the two largest underground caves in the world.

Because of this, the Riviera Maya is also flush with 'cenotes'. These are magical natural swimming holes, resulting from the collapse of limestone bedrock that exposes groundwater underneath. There are more than 6,500 different cenotes in the Yucatán Peninsula.

Veracruz, Veracruz

In 1519, Spanish explorer Hernán Cortés, understanding its mineral and seaport value, founded Veracruz. It is Mexico's oldest European-founded city. Veracruz, like all good port cities, has a history of gold and pirates and shipwrecks. It was home to a large mercantile class in the colonial period, who imported African slaves to work in the shipyards and fields.

Prior to Cortés, several indigenous cultures inhabited the region between 1300 and 400 BC. Yes, before Christ.

It's a colonial city, but major invasions over the years (the city has been invaded by the Americans, the Spanish and the French) have left her looking a little on the gritty side—but that is part of her charm. As Gary Cartwright wrote in his book about a different gulf city, *Galveston: A History of the Island*, the same could be said for Veracruz: "I often think of [her] as a ruined old bag lady in a ragged mink coat, with her last diamond hidden in her shoe."

Today, as always, she is a working port. Over 75% of all Mexican imports and exports go through Veracruz. The port is particularly important to the automotive industry. It is also an important coffee-producing region. The state of Veracruz has one of the leading economies in México, thanks to agriculture and petroleum. Petroleum was discovered offshore in the 1970s, giving the state another economic boost.

Veracruz has never been considered much of a tourist town, despite being rife with history. For example, when civil war forced Benito Juárez's government to flee México City, Juárez governed from Veracruz in 1857. The economy is strong with the size of the port of Veracruz, so perhaps it hasn't felt the need yet to tap into the tourism industry.

The cultural influence is indigenous Mexican, Spanish and Afro-Cuban, creating an ethnic dynamic you won't find elsewhere in Mexico. There is a strong Caribbean influence in the food and music.

The climate is tropical jungle—humid and hot most of the time. Rarely dipping lower than 20°C (70°F) even on the coldest of winter nights, daytime highs range in the upper-20s °C (85+°F) in the winter. In the summer, temperatures often reach mid-30s °C (95°F) and higher. The rainy season is June–October and May and June are the hottest months. Humidity will run around 80% most of the year. It's been described as oppressive—just to warn you (but they say that about Arizona, Florida and Texas during the summer, too). Be your own judge but always check these places out during the least favorable times, so you understand the worst you are getting into.

Very little English is spoken in Veracruz. Most tourism is domestic so there is no big demand for English. You will need to learn Spanish to live here.

Veracruz International Airport (VER) handles domestic and international traffic with direct flights to Houston TX. It processes about 1.6 million passengers annually, primarily to and from Mexico City, a little over an hour's flight time away.

The city of Veracruz extends into the municipality of Boca del Rio—it's all one big family and the population is in the 600,000 range, making it a decent-sized town. And yes, it's got all the box stores from Costco to Walmart to Home Depot, as well as major supermercados and incredible farmers' markets, local public markets and craft markets. It's a major port, don't forget. Everything passes through.

We would be remiss if we didn't mention the number of journalists who are killed in Veracruz state every year (mostly in Veracruz city, given it is the state capital). It has almost reached epidemic levels. Clearly, you do not want to write anything controversial here. But most of you aren't journalists and, if you are a retired reporter, just stay retired and you'll be fine.

Public hospitals include the Tarimoro General Hospital plus the Hospital Regional De Alta Especialidad de Veracruz. The private hospital, Hospital Español Veracruz, has a very good reputation. Check local directories for more information.

In summary, a historic and charming colonial city with lots to offer, both in culture and history. Lots of conveniences and an airport close by. But you'll have to be able to handle the climate (jungle hot and humid) and speak Spanish. If you can, then this is an authentic town with everything you need.

Campeche, Campeche

Mexico sure has a lot of cities with the same names as their state. That's just an aside. Campeche, Campeche, the city so nice we had to name it twice. Oh wait, that's New York. I digress.

Mayan ruins, colonial churches and great seafood make this a prime destination for enjoying colonial Mexico off the beaten path. It's all but undiscovered by tourists, again, possibly due to the climate. It's even further south.

Campeche fell to the same fate as Veracruz when the Spanish raided all the pre-Columbian gold on the coast in the 16th century. And that wall that the Spanish built around the city in the 18th century—to protect their gold stash—still stands, for the most part. More than 1,000 buildings with historical significance remain standing—a true historical city. With incredible Mayan ruins nearby—the city was actually built atop a Mayan city by the Spaniards—it was declared a UNESCO World Heritage Site in 1999.

The temperature never dips below 20°C (70°F) even on the coldest night of the year, and March–November will see highs in the mid- to upper-30s °C (upper-90s °F). In the cooler, winter months, you will still see daily highs in the low-30s °C (90s °F). Humidity is in the 77% range most of the year. It's hot. It's a jungle. Technically a tropical savanna climate, most rains fall June through October.

English is not commonly spoken in Campeche. You're getting further and further from the beaten path, but your reward is an authentic Mexican experience. You'll need to speak Spanish to live here.

The airport is the Campeche International Airport (CPE), presumably because one can fly a private plane into it from another country. There are no scheduled international flights but Aeroméxico Connect (a division of Aeroméxico) flies to Mexico City—a 90-minute flight). There are also short flights available to and from Cancún. The airport handles just under 200,000 passengers annually.

The population of Campeche is about 250,000—a reasonably sized population. Not big enough yet for Costco—although you will find one in Mérida, just 150 km (90 mi) away. There is the ubiquitous Walmart, however, and there is a Sam's Club. Plus the normal supermercados and public markets—your best bet for shopping, and most economical.

With a Caribbean influence, the palm-filled zócalo (main square) in the center of town reverberates with Marimba music at night and people meet to talk and dance. A colorful colonial gem, it's an under-the-radar spot, for now.

The public hospitals here include Hospital General de Especialidades and IMSS Centro. Hospital María Constanza is recommended as one of the best private hospitals.

Lots of history and authentic Mexican living awaits you in Campeche, if you can take the heat and humidity. Many expats who live there take off for the hottest months and visit friends and family in the north. And there is air conditioning. But make sure you know what climate you are moving to if this is your choice—it's not a climate for older people or people who have trouble breathing. The cost of living is quite low, and access to Mexico City is convenient and inexpensive. It's a pretty city with the only large warning being the climate.

Mérida, Yucatán

Mérida is a melting pot, first and foremost, of Mayan culture, adapted by Spanish, French, British, Lebanese and Dutch influence.

Approximately 60% of the city's population boasts direct Mayan heritage, the largest ratio of indigenous urban population in the country. The city was founded by the Spaniards in 1542 and built on top of a Mayan city. It is considered the oldest continuously occupied city in the Americas and has many examples of gorgeous colonial architecture.

For a brief period around the early 1900s, Mérida was said to be the city with the most millionaires in the world. It has the third-largest centro histórico in the Americas, surpassed only by Mexico City and Havana.

Mérida faces the Gulf of Mexico on northern portion of the Yucatán Peninsula, in the state of Yucatán. The city, however, is 30 km (20 mi) from the closest beach town (which is Progreso). It is 1,300 km (800 mi) east of Mexico City and is actually a little north of the capital, due to the extended peninsula.

Mérida's gastronomic history is equally as varied as its culture. Yucatán food is a mixture of Mayan, European, Caribbean and Mexican (with a splash of Middle Eastern thrown in). It can be differentiated from other Mexican foods by the amount of fruit that is used in main courses.

Mérida is unquestionably one of the most interesting cities in Mexico, with a vibrant culture and many conveniences, but her climate can be severe.

In fact, the climate is the rub for most expats, although there is a strong expat community there. They must leave in the summer. Your average highs, even in the coldest winter months, are almost 30°C (90°F) and climb well into the mid- to upper-30s °C (95+°F) from March–October.

This is not a climate for sissies. Humidity runs 65–75% depending on the season, and the rainy season runs June through September. It's a tropical climate—the rains are like monsoons and can be quite spectacular. Hurricanes occur most often in September and October.

While there is a (rapidly) growing expat community here, you really do want to learn to speak Spanish or you'll miss the best things about living here. In the tourist restaurants, museums and hotels, you will find English spoken. Venture off the beaten path and you'll at least want to speak some Spanish.

At a population nearing one million, the city has everything you would expect. The cultural heritage is intact with museums and careful restorations of 16th century buildings—but there are also many modern shopping malls and car dealerships. It's a city. Tourism is increasing (by leaps and bounds) and more and more expats are heading to town, often to refurbish and restore old homes in the city center. The trick? They go to one of the beach towns for July and August where they get a breeze, as the Mayans were known to do. Or head north. But one way or the other, they get out of dodge.

Manuel Crescencio Rejón International Airport (MID) at Mérida handles planes as large as 747s and is open 24 hours a day. That should give you some idea. There are direct flights from Canada and the US in the winter—these routes are more limited in frequency through the warmer summer months. It does handle more than 2 million passengers a year and is one of the larger airports in Mexico. As more tourists arrive, more direct flights will open up.

If you're an expat moving to Mérida, there are a couple of areas worth checking out. Many expats buy old colonial homes in the town center and restore them. There are some affluent neighborhoods like Santiago to the west and north of the Plaza Grande and Santa Ana, a burgeoning art district, with galleries and museums. Many expats live in the north part of town. But really, depends on what you want in a neighborhood. I'd act quickly though—all these gringos are driving the prices up. It's one of the newest cool spots.

There are, of course, the incredible local Mexican public markets, farmers' markets and organic markets in town. And the big box stores—Home Depot, Sam's Club, multiple Walmarts and Costco. Not just any Costco, however—it's likely the only Costco in the world with a cenote.

The underground cavern was discovered when they were building the structure and it was terraced, landscaped and lit. Bravo, Costco!

For public health care, Hospital General Regional Lic Ignacio Garcia Tellez IMSS (that's a mouthful) is a popular choice. The better private hospitals include Hospital Médica Sur and ABC Medical Center.

In summary, Mérida is a great place to live if you're looking for a culturally active city with lots of history and lots of opportunity. Prices are still reasonable, but there should be an up-tick in property value over the next few years. A city in its own right, it has everything you'd ever need. Although connected to the resort area of Cancún by a superhighway, it is eons away from Cancún in ambiance and history. If you can get away for the worst of the hot and humid summer months, this could be quite a pleasant place to live.

Cancún, Quintana Roo

Cancún was literally a coconut plantation with three residents when the National Fund for Tourism decided it would make a good resort. Development began in 1970 and today, alongside Acapulco, it is one of the best-known tourist resorts in the country.

Situated on the tip of the Yucatán Peninsula, its shores face the Caribbean Sea, part of the larger Gulf of Mexico. It is just north of the Riviera Maya, just 1,300 km (800 mi) east and slightly north of Mexico City—as the crow flies. By car, it is 1,600 km (1,000 mi).

Full of white sand beaches, the location was chosen by a computer. The government input factors like average temperatures, beach quality and accessibility—and Cancún was born.

Being a beach town, it's humid. The humidity dips to 75% at night but is rarely below 85% in the day. Winter weather is pleasant. November to April averages highs below 30°C (mid-80s) and 30+ °C (90+°F) the rest of the year. There is usually a light breeze from the ocean but the humidity ups the stakes. Air conditioning is a must. Rainy season (and the hottest season) is May to October with regular, heavy tropical showers. The last major hurricanes to hit Cancún were Gilbert (1988) and Wilma (2005).

Cancún has grown from a sleepy little beach town into a mega tourist destination and you can certainly get along with no Spanish. But you may wish to learn it in order to interact with the locals. There is plenty of opportunity, with the correct visas, for expats to open businesses in the tourism industry. Destination wedding planning is a large industry—between Cancún and the Riviera Maya, more than 46,000 weddings were held in 2017. From five-star restaurants to diving tours to website builders—the demand is there. The international airport at Cancún handled more than 32 million passengers in 2023—process that from a retail point of view.

And it's a stunning modern airport with direct flights to many places in the world. At 23+ million passengers in 2017—Cancún International Airport (CUN) is the country's second-busiest airport after Mexico City's Benito Juárez. From the airport, shuttles or taxis will take you anywhere you're going on the Riviera Maya.

The population of Cancún is approximately 900,000—a city in its own right. It's grown exponentially since its creation but the infrastructure is good, being newer and being a major jewel for the tourism agencies. There are a variety of diving adventures to be had, from exploring the spectacular Cancún Underwater Museum (MUSA) with more than 400 sculptures, to diving the Great Mayan Reef (the second largest in the world). And ruins and history are a short bus ride away. You'll find spectacular dining with food prepared by the top European chefs.

All the conveniences of home are here, from upscale movie theaters showing just-released movies in English to all the typical box stores—Costco, Sam's Club, Walmart, Home Depot and many large upscale Mexican grocery and department store chains—also, many organic and farmers' markets and craft markets. You won't hurt for shopping in this town.

There aren't a lot of expats in Cancún, proportionately, considering the city is almost a million people. It's hard to nail down numbers but the entire state of Quintana Roo is becoming trendy and reports are seeing a 10–15% increase in immigration applications. Estimates say 10–15,000 expats live in Cancún year-round, with 2,000 new applications for residency coming in every year.

Many expats seem to live in the hotel zone by the beach. Which makes sense—you're moving to be close to the ocean and it's unquestionably the safest part of Cancún. They will do whatever it takes to protect the tourism zone, as it is the only reason Cancún exists. But, while you'll find great beach life, lots of restaurants and tourist shops, you won't find much of what you'll need for living there.

The box stores and big grocery stores are all in town in the general area of the Saint-Tropez neighborhood, which also houses some expat residences. In any event, you'll need a car to live here—having been built in the automobile-friendly 1970s, it's not a walking town.

Public hospitals include Hospital General de Cancún and Hospiten Cancún. As a major medical tourism destination, you have your choice of top rate private hospitals, including Hospital Amerimed.

In summary, living in Cancún—unless you live outside the hotel zone—is really not a Mexican experience but is a very pleasant one. If you do live outside the hotel zone, you will want to learn a little Spanish. That said, this place has the weather, it has the airport, and you can experience all of the conveniences without any of the effort to assimilate that is required in some other towns. If you can handle the heat and humidity (especially in the summer), are an avid diver or if you want to start a gringo business, this is the place for you. Most houses outside the Mexican areas are priced in US dollars and this can be a bit of a deterrent for Canadians and Europeans. US currency is widely accepted but you may always legally pay in the peso equivalent.

Playa del Carmen, Quintana Roo (with a nod to Cozumel)

Just 50 km (30 mi) south of Cancún lies Playa del Carmen, or Playa as it is commonly known. Once a sleepy fishing village, it is one of the fastest growing regions in all of Mexico.

And it's always been a little more laid back than Cancún. A small village, it only became popular when the island of Cozumel became a tourist destination (Playa is where the ferry to Cozumel embarks from the mainland). With its rapid growth have come many resorts and high-end condominium developments on the beach, yet is has retained its Mexican ambiance.

With a lower cost of living than either Cancún or Cabo San Lucas, Playa del Carmen is still pricier than inland locations. It's the beach—you pay for access to the ocean.

The nearby Island of Cozumel, separated from Playa by 20 km (12 mi) of water, is a world-class diving destination and a tourism draw itself.

As an aside, in 1861, then-US president Abraham Lincoln floated the idea of buying Cozumel to relocate freed US slaves offshore. Sheesh. The idea was dismissed by Mexican president Benito Juárez. The economy of the island is tied to tourism and diving, and it's a close day trip from Playa.

The climate is a little more moderate than one might expect, with highs generally running in the mid- to upper-20s °C (75–85°F) during the winter months, and reaching 30°C (90°F) during the summer months of May–September. Relative humidity hits 80% most days of the year. It's a muggy, tropical climate—and hot in the summer. But some people like that. And, on the bright side, it never gets below about 18°C (65°F), so that's nice.

The rainy season runs from May to October (always inclusive) and, while steady enough, rainfall doubles (read: deluge) in September and October, which is also when most hurricanes hit.

Most restaurants, especially near the beach, will have menus in English and Spanish, and they will speak English in the hotels and some boutiques and galleries. But to live here, you want to learn some Spanish, as it is more of a Mexican town than Cancún. It really is quite an authentic Mexican beach town, if that's what you're after.

Cancún International Airport (CUN) is the second busiest airport in Mexico and is less than an hour's drive to the north. There are many shuttles from Playa to the airport at all hours of the day and night—although it is always recommended that road travel in Mexico be done during daylight hours when possible.

Alternately, the Cozumel International Airport (CZM) is just a ferry ride away and provides direct flights to many US and Canadian locations, being a tourism and diving mecca.

The population of Playa del Carmen is 300,000+ and growing rapidly. The expat community is also expanding as more tourists choose Playa over the party life in Cancún. It's home to several PGA courses and has been featured in some TV shows—*The Real Housewives of Vancouver* and *The Amazing Race*, among others). US dollars are widely accepted in Playa and preferred by many businesses—a bit of a deterrent for Canadians and Europeans but this is true of most of the Riviera Maya and certainly in Cancún.

Most expats tend to look in Playa Centro for living space—a large central area with lots of beach. After all, the beach is why you're here, right? You'll find Sam's Club and Walmart, but for Costco, you'll have to go north to Cancún. There are plenty of local and farmers' markets, as well as supermercados such as Mega and Chedraui. And all the conveniences of Cancún are less than an hour away.

Public hospitals include Hospital General de Playa del Carmen (are you seeing a pattern here) and the #18 IMSS Hospital. Private hospitals include another branch of the renowned Hospital Amerimed.

In summary, Playa del Carmen is a much more authentic Mexican beach town than Cancún but without as many conveniences. Still, it may suit many as it has less of a party vibe. The weather is still tropical muggy and oppressive in the summer and you'll want to get away but, as you've read, that's the case in many beach towns. Overall, Playa seems like a good choice for beach lovers who don't want to be face-to-face with tourists every day.

Akumal and Tulum, Quintana Roo

Akumal doesn't have a lot of history—it was founded in 1958 as a town for scuba divers. So, it has only existed for 70 years.

Tulum, on the other hand, was a pre-Columbian walled Mayan city that served as a port. Tulum has the best coastal Mayan ruins in Mexico and is quite a popular tourist destination. It is also easily reached from Cancún, which is about 100 km (60 mi) north.

Akumal and Tulum are such very different cities, but only 25 km (16 mi) apart. Situated on the very southern end of the Riviera Maya in Quintana Roo state, Tulum is the southernmost of the two towns.

Which town you prefer really depends on your personal style. If this is your chosen climate and geographical location, which kind of environment do you want to live in—Tulum rustic or Akumal modern? Tulum is funkier and more rustic while Akumal has high-rise condos on the beach.

The climate of the two towns is almost identical—hot and humid. In the winter months, highs hover around 30°C (90°F) and in the summer months, the area sees highs in the mid-30s °C (95+°F). Lows are consistently in the low-20s °C (70s °F).

One advantage of these temperatures is that the ocean is always nice and warm, never going below 26°C (79°F) in the winter and reaching 30°C (90°F) in the summer.

The rainy season is May to October with September seeing the most rainfall. And make no mistake, this is tropical rain and can be quite heavy at times (albeit warm). The humidity varies quite a bit. It hovers around 60% from December to March but reaches oppressive levels of 100% humidity from May-September.

Be sure to visit during this time period if you have any desire to live here—you need to be here during the hottest time to make an honest decision.

Not everyone you encounter will speak English, although it will be more common in retail outlets and restaurants in the tourist areas. You'll want to learn some Spanish if this is where you plan to move. A little Spanish goes a long way in towns like this.

You'll be using either Cancún International Airport (CUN) or Cozumel International Airport (CZM)—both a couple of hours away by land, but offering many direct international flights.

Akumal is almost like a suburb of Tulum—it has less than 2,500 residents, while Tulum has nearly 50,000 (and is growing quickly).

Tulum has become quite trendy and there are a lot of eco-friendly resorts. You'll find matcha smoothie bowls and kombucha at boho beach bars and New York-style mezcal bars in the jungle. It's Instagram-ready, for now at least.

There are some services in Tulum, but you'll be heading to Playa and occasionally Cancún for major purchases. No big box stores but plenty of local markets and supermercados.

There is a 24-hour private hospital in Tulum for emergencies and a medical center in Akumal. For IMSS or INSABI coverage, one needs to travel to Playa del Carmen.

In summary, if you're looking to live in an up-and-coming area, love to dive and want to be in a smaller town—if you can handle the humidity, Tulum and Akumal are both good choices, although Tulum is the trendy sister.

You'll drive to go to the airport (or take a shuttle) and you'll drive to do major shopping. You need to consider how often you'll be doing this and will it become a chore—as well as the effect of the humidity on your day-to-day life.

Chapter 6:

Colonial highlands north

San Luis Potosí, San Miguel de Allende, Guanajuato, Querétaro

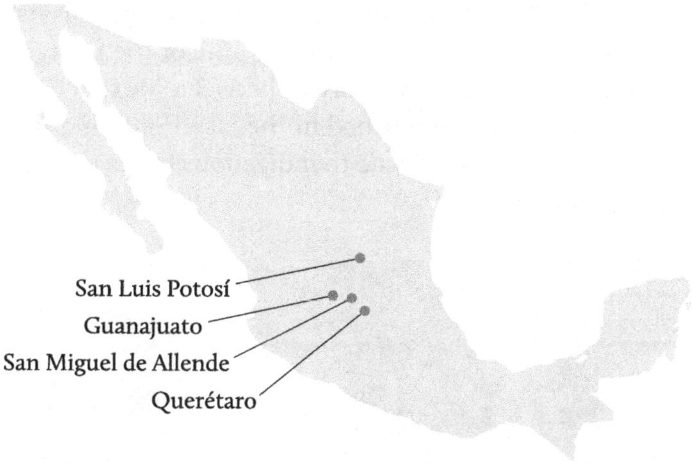

Year-round temperate climates with low humidity, crisp air and good infrastructure are all good reasons to choose Mexico's colonial highlands. Sure, the beaches are fantastic, especially in the winter, but expats who can't handle the humidity are making mountain Mexico their home.

The northern swatch of the colonial highlands (north of Mexico City) had silver and lots of it. The Spanish made quick work of that—there is very little left. But there is tons of history and culture, and gorgeous old colonial architecture.

The cuisine of this area relies largely on pork—don't miss carnitas—a shredded pork (for tacos) that is simmered in pork fat. Yes, meat fried in meat fat. Bad for your arteries but crunchy and good. And the region is heavy on dairy—rice pudding (*arroz con leche*) is a favorite, as is cajeta (goats' milk caramel).

San Luis Potosí, San Luis Potosí

See, they did it again (city and state with the same name). San Luis Potosí the city, commonly called SLP or San Luis, is named after Louis the IX from France. It's now one of the main industrial centers of Mexico, lying halfway between Mexico City and the US border. It was established in the late 1500s as a mining center but had long been home to indigenous tribes prior to the Spanish conquests.

It's an attractive colonial city that was listed as a UNESCO World Heritage Site in 2010. For a time in 1863, during the French invasion of Mexico, San Luis Potosí served as the capital of the republican government under President Benito Juárez. And it was a gold and silver mining hub from the 16th–19th centuries. Today, it's a thriving city with more than a million people.

San Luis is 400 km (250 mi) north and slightly east of Mexico City—about a five-hour drive or a one-hour flight. At 1,850 m (6,000 ft) above sea level, the climate is semi-arid. The temperature is moderate with highs ranging from the low-20s (70+°F) in the winter and only reaching about 28 °C (82°F) in the summer. Lows run from the mid-teens in the summer (60°F) to the single digits—as low as 5°C (40°F) in the middle of a cold winter night. January is usually the coldest month.

It's got a very interesting side. Not far from town, eccentric English artist James Edward created a most unusual garden in his home in the municipality of Xilitla. Las Pozas (The Pools), as it is called, is 80 acres of towering surrealist sculptures presiding over natural ponds. Some of the names of the sculptures: *The House on Three Floors Which Will in Fact Have Five or Four or Six*, *The House with a Roof like a Whale* and *The Staircase to Heaven.*

At one point, he had as many as 29,000 orchids on display. Las Pozas cost Edward upwards of US$5.5 million to build. It's worth seeing. Multiple times.

Rainy season is May through October, like much of the country. Humidity is barely present all winter and only reaches 50% in the height of the summer. Overall a very pleasant climate, if you can handle the cool nights in January—or hit the beach that month.

This is an authentic Mexican city and its language is Spanish. That said, there are some English speakers, as many US companies have branches here. It's the main industrial center of central Mexico.

Ponciano Arriaga International Airport (SLP) handles more than 700,000 passengers a year, many of whom are business travelers. There are plenty of direct flights to Dallas and Houston and it's less than an hour to fly to Mexico City to connect to European and Canadian destinations.

With a population of more than a million people, this is a proper city with all the conveniences. There are a number of expats who have been sent down by their companies—they tend to congregate together, and the families, knowing they are short-term residents, don't assimilate much.

It has all the box stores and all the big Mexican chains—Costco, Home Depot, Sam's Club, Chedraui, Liverpool and more. You won't want for anything here. There are many faces to the town.

The standard public hospitals are here including Hospital General ISSSTE and Hospital General #50 IMSS. There are many good private hospitals (international companies abound)—among them, Hospital de Las Américas San Luis and Hospital Lomas de San Luis Internacional get top marks.

Overall, San Luis Potosí has a lot to offer. The weather is good, there are attractive things to do, it's a large city with good access to the Mexico City airport, if its own airport is somewhat lacking. It has a large number of educational institutions and research stations—so the people you meet will be interesting. If you don't mind the slight inconvenience of the air travel (there are always trade-offs), this is probably one of the best colonial cities to choose as home.

San Miguel de Allende, Guanajuato

San Miguel de Allende was founded by the Spanish in 1541 but later became the first municipality declared independent of Spanish rule, during the Mexican War of Independence (1810–1821). It became a quiet, calm place frequented by rich Mexicans because of its proximity to the hot springs. It's right smack in the middle of Mexico's cradle of independence and, like Guanajuato, it's got rich history.

After WWII, the returning GIs in America discovered that their education grants went further in Mexico and began using them to attend the US-accredited art school, the Instituto Allende. The tourism industry in San Miguel was born.

Today, the bustling town of 150,000 (approximately 15,000 are gringos) is home to stunning art galleries, intriguing stores and international restaurants. At the same time, vendors meander down cobblestone paths with their burros (donkeys). There is a large expat population and they are organized. In fact, it's so large that in the Wikipedia listing for San Miguel, the first subtitle under *Culture* is *Foreign influence*.

It is truly a beautiful town—and a town that has been somewhat created by San Miguel's tourism department, but has a bona fide history. The streets are cobblestone (most of them) and there are a lot of steep hills, yet they tout it as a walking town. When we lived there (2012–14), it was getting busy on weekends and it is even busier today. It's one of the most domestically visited destinations in all of Mexico for tourism and many Chilangos (Mexico City residents) have weekend homes in town.

There isn't a lot of middle class in San Miguel—although that might be changing among the expats. But there are very wealthy foreigners here, and very wealthy Mexicans. And a disproportionate number of houses with dirt floors and tarpaulin roofs, mostly outside the Centro.

There truly is some incredible architecture in this town. But no denying the expats drive the economy, as do the wealthy Chilangos. There are boutique hotels and four-star restaurants and lots of New York prices. In fact, a large number of expats are New Yorkers. And in the summer, you'll find many Texas 'sunbirds' in residence.

It's likely the climate that attracts them. It can get cool in the winter and, having lived there two years, it did go below freezing overnight several times in January and February. In the day, it warms up nicely in the winter and is almost always sunny. Lows will run in the lower single digits at night in the winter, with highs in the 25°C (77°F) range. April and May are the warmest months, reaching highs into the lows 30s °C (90s °F) and humidity of 50–60% year-round. It is a mid-altitude desert climate with lots of sun and cooler nighttime temperatures. The rainy season is May to September, with late afternoon and evening storms.

It's located about 275 km (170 mi) northeast of Mexico City. There are no direct buses from Mexico City's airport to San Miguel, but you can take connecting buses, changing in Querétaro. Otherwise, you can take a shared shuttle for US$75.

There are closer, smaller airports (León and Querétaro) with direct flights only to the southern US—if you are from Canada or Europe, you'll want to fly from Mexico City.

Unfortunately (or fortunately—depending on your perspective), you don't have to learn Spanish to hang out with the gringos in this town. And most of the expats don't speak much, it seems. Although those who make the effort to learn are rewarded with a new circle of friends—Mexicans who own stores and restaurants in town for whom English is not preferred.

In bilingual social groups, you'll often find a mix of the two languages being spoken. A sentence in Spanish, then a sentence in English, back and forth at will. If you're lucky enough to be part of a group like this, your Spanish will improve exponentially.

The population, as noted, is about 175,000 with around 17,500 or so expats—most of whom live inside the city limits. The town attracts artists, musicians and writers. It has community theatre. Live music can be found almost any night of the week. The local newspaper, *Atención*, is printed in Spanish and English, and has lots of information.

Expats live everywhere but are noticeably dense in Centro, San Antonio and Guadiana. Inside the periférico (the ring-road around town) is preferred, although there are some areas and gated communities just outside town that are well-populated.

Celaya, just 50 km (35 mi) away, has the ubiquitous four box stores—Costco, Home Depot, Sam's Club and Walmart—but in the other direction, Querétaro has so much more. And, Celeya can have a great deal of violent crime. San Miguel itself has a Soriana and a La Comer for large supermarkets and many smaller mini-mercados, some specializing in imported foods. And now, City Market (an upscale supermarket) has come to San Miguel. There's a Liverpool (department store), and many local Mexican produce and meat markets. The Tuesday tianguis (market) is huge—and is repeated in a smaller format on Sundays. There is an organic (hipster-like) market on Saturdays in town, and several times a year there are large craft fairs. There is also a good artisan market for Mexican folk art, handicrafts and rugs.

The public hospital system in San Miguel includes Hospital General Dr Felipe G Dobarganes. With a wealthy gringo population, the private care is good and includes Hospital Joya San Miguel and Hopitales MAC.

You can take a class in oil painting, guitar playing or *How to Write Your Memoirs*. There are many social charitable events (more than 100 expat non-governmental organizations) and always an eclectic array of seminars and workshops to pick from. There are a lot of retired people here. One friend (who loves it) regularly refers to it as 'elder camp'. But there's everything a retired person could want. Yoga? Reiki? Looking for good naturopathy? Or just a relaxing coffee at Starbucks? You get the idea. You don't have to change your lifestyle much to live in this town.

It's an easy transition from north of the border to San Miguel and an easy place for a gringo to live. There is plenty of Mexican culture on display throughout the year, thanks to it being a popular tourist town. Which also means there are plenty of celebrations and fiestas and general noise, but it's worth it. They do know how to fiesta in this town. There is medical care in English—most everything is available in English—and the big box stores are close by. Overall, a good town to land in and you might decide to stay.

Guanajuato (city), Guanajuato

During the colonial period, Guanajuato was an extremely influential city due to fortunes made from mining. In 1558 a big silver vein was discovered in Guanajuato and the La Valenciana Mine produced nearly a third of all silver in the world for the next 250 years. In the 16th century, it was the richest city in all of Mexico.

Along with other towns, Guanajuato is located in the region known as Mexico's cradle of independence. And this city is a living history lesson. The stories just go on and on. There's an old building in town, built as a grain storage facility (Alhóndiga de Granaditas)—the taking of this building was the opening volley in the Siege of Guanajuato (1810). This was the first confrontation in the Mexican War of Independence (from Spain)—a war that would take 11 years to win.

Long story short, the four amigos, Hidalgo, Allende, Aldama and Jiménez took the granary but, less than a year later, each of their four heads would hang in cages from the exterior corners of the building. And their heads would hang there for 10 years, until Mexico achieved independence. The Spanish were brutal. At the end of the war, the heads were moved to Mexico City, where they are buried under El Ángel (Monumento a la Independencia). So, you can see how important this town is to Mexican history—and that story is just a minor part of it all.

Guanajuato is a colorful colonial city with stunning architecture (due to its mineral wealth during that period). The colonial architecture includes some of the best baroque examples in the New World—these buildings are simply jaw-dropping.

Home to the mummy museum (bodies that have been dug up and put on display to recoup unpaid graveyard fees, I'm not kidding), the kissing alley (a charming love story) and the world-famous Guanajuato International Film Festival (GIFF) every July, this university town has a lot going for it. Even its name has a neat story behind it—Guanajuato means 'place of frogs' in the local indigenous language—and that makes the frog the official pet of Guanajuato City.

The climate is moderate—I hate to sound like a broken record, but this is like most of the colonial cities at higher altitudes. You don't get the longer term sweltering heat, but do have to put up with some quite cool nights in the deep of winter. They don't last long.

Guanajuato enjoys temperature highs of (more or less) the low-20s °C (70s °F) in the winter and upper-20s °C (80s+°F) in the summer. Lows in the winter go to single digits but rarely dip below 7 or 8°C (upper-40s °F) and, in the summer, lows run a pleasant 15°C (60°F).

The rainy season is May to October with most rain falling in July. Humidity runs around 50% during the winter and up to the lower 70% range in the summer, so it can get a little muggy on the worst days. Elevation is 2,000 m (6,600 ft).

This is a Mexican town. There are some expats, but Spanish is spoken everywhere except in the most touristy of spots. Again, you will find many middle-class Mexicans who do speak English, but as their second language. You'd be hard pressed to take full advantage of this wonderful town without at least learning some of the language.

Guanajuato International Airport (BJX), also known as Del Bajío International Airport, handles 3 million passengers a year, but remains an easy-to-use facility. It's an important connector to Mexico City with direct flights to many major US cities. It also offers one-stop flights from major Canadian cities, that stop being Mexico City and the airline being Aeroméxico. It is situated between León and Guanajuato.

The population is about 200,000 and the town is both the state capital and a university town. It's got a lot of culture and art. Aside from GIFF, the renowned Festival Internacional Cervantino (El Cervantino) is hosted by the University of Guanajuato every year in October. The university is the oldest in all of Latin America and was first opened in the 18th century as a Jesuit school for children. And, of course, last but not least, the city is the birthplace of Diego Rivera.

Centro is a great spot to live and many expats do. They also seem to gravitate toward the Marfil neighborhood, with large, Spanish-colonial houses—and to La Presa, with large homes and water views.

I'm afraid that for box stores, you'll be heading to León, about an hour's drive away. At well over a million people, León's got the four horsemen (Costco, Sam's, Walmart and Home Depot). León is famous for its leather work and full of factory outlets with shoes and bags, so worth the drive. You will find all the major supermarkets (Mega, La Comer, Soriana) and local Mexican markets right in Guanajuato.

The public hospital systems includes the ISSSTE Clinic Hospital and the Hospital General de Guanajuato. Private hospitals include Unidad Médica and Medical City Hospital. Check local directories for more choices.

In summary, this is a historical town full of stunning buildings and a university that has a student body of more than 10,000 at the main campus. You know that university towns are usually great places to live. The climate is good, there are lots of conveniences as well as lots of culture, history and art. You'll have to drive for an hour if you need to go to Costco or the like. The expats are here, but not in droves, so you'll have to speak Spanish. If you can manage that, this could be your town.

Querétaro (city), Querétaro

See? There they go again with the repeated names. Querétaro is the capital of the state, located about 200 km (120 mi) northwest of Mexico City. The area was settled in 200 AD by Mesoamerican groups heading north. It was populated by the Otomí, sedentary urban dwellers and also the Chichimeca, who were semi-nomadic people.

And then along came the Spanish, as they did. Enough said.

Considered part of Mexico's cradle of independence, the city has a strong history and charming historic center. Emperor Maximilian surrendered in Querétaro in 1867 and was subsequently executed by firing squad. The Mexican Constitution was written in Querétaro in 1917.

It is, of course, a UNESCO World Heritage Site (1996). But make no mistake, outside the center, this is a modern, modern city. Aside from having one of the most modern stadiums in all of Mexico, it is also home to the most prestigious universities.

The last decade has shown huge economic growth in the city—and the industrialization has promoted a 3.5% growth in population per year. The major industries include IT, parts manufacturing and food processing. It's a happening city with talk of high-speed rail to Mexico City. Querétaro is located about 200 km (120 mi) northwest of Mexico City, a short flight or a three-hour drive on a very good toll road.

The region has also become a wine-growing area of note. The second largest wine-growing region in Mexico (after Baja), it has attracted the likes of Spain's Freixenet—and cheese and wine tours are the new Querétaro experience.

The climate is much like that of most high-elevation colonial cities. At 1,800 m (6,000 ft) above sea level, the nights dip into single digits in the winter but reach highs in the mid-20s °C (75°F) during the day. Summer isn't overly hot, rarely reaching highs of 30°C (90°F) and, then, only in the hottest of months.

The rainy season is May to October and the humidity ranges from 40–60%, which is reasonable and quite bearable. The elevation mitigates everything. It can feel a little muggy and warm in May when you're looking at 30°C (90°F) and 60% humidity but it doesn't last. One of the more moderate climates around. I'm sure you're starting to see why people like the colonial cities—the weather is not as dramatic (I'm being kind—I find the beach heat unbearable in the summer).

With the second largest per capita GDP after Monterrey, Querétaro is a working, modern industrial city with large operations by many international firms such as Bombardier Aerospace, Samsung and General Electric. There is a working expat population here and smaller pockets of retired expats.

Places that normally deal with foreigners—restaurants, hotels and airport services—will speak English but, for the most part, it's a Spanish-speaking city. You'll find gringo communities where English only is spoken, but these tend to be more company-oriented and populated by short-term residents. That said, these working expats often create newcomer groups or Facebook pages that are invaluable for gleaning information and recommendations.

Querétaro Intercontinental Airport (QRO) handles more than 1.5 million passengers a year and that number is growing. There are direct flights to some US cities—including Chicago, Detroit, Atlanta and Dallas—but Canadians and Europeans will need to connect on a short flight to Mexico City (or take an airport shuttle to Mexico City).

The population of Querétaro is more than 2.5 million people and it has grown exponentially in recent years. It's large enough to have everything you want (and more). The thriving economy ensures there will be upscale and trendy products available in many stores.

For the convenience of shopping—and I mean everything from groceries, to clothing, to furniture—it's one of the best cities in Mexico, in my opinion. If you like to shop in person, that is. Alternately, almost anything you need is available to anywhere in Mexico via online shopping (see *Chapter 24: Handy guides*).

A number of expats settle in Juriquilla, a residential area just north of the city (30 minutes from the historic center). Mirador, Jurica and Milenio are also popular areas. And you'll always find expats restoring colonial buildings right in the historic center.

Querétaro has all the box stores you'd ever want—Office Depot, Costco, Home Depot, Sam's Club and more. And all of the supermarkets—from City Market (my favorite) to Superama to

Chedraui. The selection here for shopping is almost as good as Mexico City and certainly has nowhere near the traffic.

There are extremely upscale stores at the Antea LifeStyle Center shopping mall, including Louis Vuitton, Dolce & Gabbana—and a Ferrari dealership. You do the math.

Public hospitals here include Hospital General de Querétaro and ISSTE General Hospital. This city has many private hospitals, including the top rated Star Medica and Hospital Ángeles.

In summary, this is an affluent town that is growing by leaps and bounds and able to sustain its growth. The city attributes its cleanliness and livability to its policy of maintaining infrastructure and creating parks and other pleasant public spaces. You can't beat that attitude for a municipal government.

The weather is moderate, the access to Mexico City and its airport is convenient and there's everything you need right there. As far as colonial cities go, this one rates high—it's a decent place to live and, if you buy a home, it is almost certain to be a good investment.

Chapter 7:

Colonial highlands west

Guadalajara, Chapala-Ajijic, Morelia, Pátzcuaro

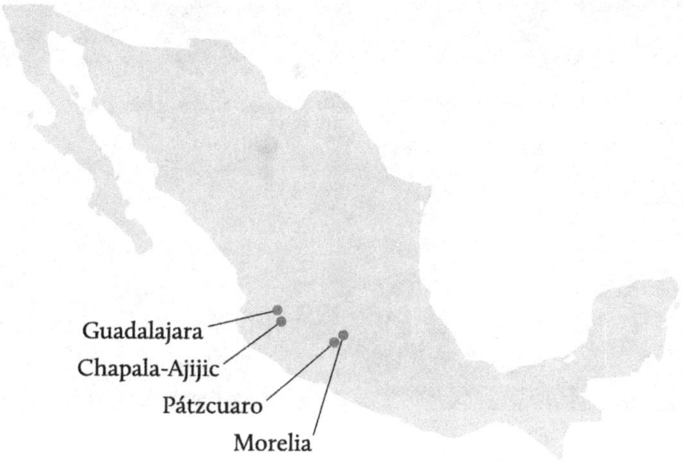

Heading slightly to the west of Mexico City (and running from slightly north to almost even), we find more stunning colonial cities with architecture and history and culture—and the weather is all so similar and so temperate. And, for the most part, you'll find burros being led down cobblestone streets, cathedrals dating back hundreds of years. These cities all have expat populations and proximity to the Mexico City airport—which is not to be minimized if getting out of town is on your agenda.

Guadalajara, Jalisco

The second largest city in the country (next to Mexico City), Guadalajara is known as the land of tequila and mariachi. Not a bad reputation. But it's also got history, culture and fantastic architecture. The state of Jalisco is home to a significant expat population, encompassing Guadalajara, Ajijic—on Lake Chapala—and Puerto Vallarta.

Guadalajara is situated in the central region of the state, a little more than 400 km (250 mi) northwest of Mexico City.

It had a large indigenous population of Chichimecs when the Spanish invaded in the 16th century. The village of Guadalajara barely survived the Mixtón War (1540–42) and the locals attributed that survival to the Archangel Michael, the patron of the city.

It's a historical, colonial town with incredible architecture and it played a large role in the Mexican War of Independence. A diversified city, today it is home to the world-renowned Guadalajara International Film Festival—which sees more than 100,000 attendees—and the Guadalajara International Book Fair, one of the largest literary trade fairs in the world.

Called *The Pearl of the West*, Guadalajara is a modern city that has retained the traditions of Jalisco. It has six universities, two culinary institutes and a thriving art scene. The suburbs of Tlaquepaque offers upscale dining and art gallery opportunities while nearby Tonalá is a center for glass manufacturing as well as paper mâché art.

It has a moderate climate, very similar to Querétaro (however, as a note of caution, the summers are more humid in this location). At 1,500 m (5,000 ft) above sea level, the elevation mitigates the temperatures. The nights dip into single digits (as low as 4°C, or low-40s °F) in the worst of the winter but reach highs in the mid-20s °C (75°F) during the day. The summer temperatures rarely break 30°C (90°F), but the humidity can be as high as 75%. The largest freshwater lake in Mexico, Lake Chapala, is approximately 50 km (30 mi) south of the city.

Again, in areas that have a high rate of transient foreigners—tourist attractions, hotels, airports—people will speak English. And because it's an educated population, many will speak English as their second language. But this is a Mexican city and the first language is Spanish. Learning the language, even just the basics, will take you a long way. And there's something to be said about immersing yourself in a Spanish-speaking city this large. Everywhere you go, you will overhear Spanish conversation. Eventually, it will start to seep in by osmosis and will help you to learn. There is, however, an English-language newspaper, *The Guadalajara Reporter*. It has been in business for 40 years serving not only Guadalajara but also Ajijic, Lake Chapala and Puerto Vallarta (more of a state newspaper).

Miguel Hidalgo y Costilla Guadalajara International Airport (GDL) is located 16 km (10 mi) to the south of the city, conveniently about halfway to Ajijic and Lake Chapala. It's one of the nicest, and easiest, airports I have been in. Not too big and well-organized. It handles nearly 18 million passengers a year, ranking third busiest behind Mexico City and Cancún.

While it has direct flights to most major American cities, Canada- or Europe-bound passengers will need to connect via a short flight to Mexico City.

The metropolitan population of Guadalajara is 5.2 million (the city itself is 1.5 million). Think Toronto or Chicago for comparison. If you like cities but find Mexico City too large, this is the spot for you. Traffic is abominable (think Toronto or Chicago).

Colonia Americana in Guadalajara, very close to the Centro, is enjoying a resurgence and becoming gentrified. Other popular places to live include the suburb of Tlaquepaque with its art galleries and shops—and Providencia, with its upscale boutiques and trendy cafés.

Of course, every shopping experience you could imagine is here. All the big stores—in fact, there are actually two Costco locations in Guadalajara. But don't be so blinded by all the convenience and bling that you miss the local markets. And Driscoll's has a huge, covered operation just south of the city where they grow blueberries and raspberries for export around the world. Trust me, you have never seen such big berries. And do not miss the Tonalá craft market, held on the main street for miles and miles with hundreds of vendors every Tuesday and Saturday. It can be overwhelming but is not to be missed.

Just 50 km (35 mi) northwest of Guadalajara is the municipality of Tequila—yes, where tequila comes from. Much like the Champagne region of France, this is a controlled liquor that comes from only one region. The outskirts of town are dotted with distinctive fields of blue agave—the plant from which tequila is made—and once you've seen them, they are instantly recognizable.

Public hospitals include Hospital General de Occidente and Hospital Civil. This city has some of the best hospitals in the country. Private hospitals include Hospital Mexico Americano and Hospital Ramón Garibay. There are many specialty hospitals here, check local directories for more information.

In summary, a nice, big, clean city if city life is for you. Lots of art, culture, history and architecture. Lots to do, great shopping, wonderful restaurants and a relatively moderate climate. Mexico's largest freshwater lake is less than an hour away, if you'd like a weekend house or summer cottage. What's not to like?

Chapala and Ajijic, Jalisco (on Lake Chapala)

Until the arrival of the Spanish in 1535, the area was populated by nomadic tribes, primarily the Coca people. The area was colonized by the Franciscans (and thus many of the churches and monasteries) but Ajijic was made popular in the 1920s by European artists and intellectuals who valued the climate and ambiance of the lakeside location.

They're pretty much one town, stretching into each other on the north shore of Lake Chapala, a little more than 50 km (30 mi) south of Guadalajara. Lake Chapala is Mexico's largest freshwater lake.

Despite being joined at the hip, the two towns (in the same municipality) remain very different in ambiance. Chapala is a working town, primarily Mexican, with a smaller number of expats (and a larger population). Ajijic, on the other hand, has a very organized gringo community and they control the economy. While it is still Mexican—and beautiful colonial buildings abound—the restaurants and stores are all influenced by expat wants and needs.

Chapala is larger and quite attractive in its own right. If you want to specifically avoid the large gringo population, you should live here. You'll be much more immersed in the Mexican lifestyle and you'll still have all the conveniences of a gringo town just 15 minutes away.

There are many who are 'snowbirds' and don't live there all year, but that will be changing as more people retire. I've heard that in the winter, the town swells to 50% expats, and that's substantial. It's a small town—about 15,000—and with the higher gringo population during winter, many services become strained. There's a Walmart here, right in town. In a town this size. So that tells you something. But, to be fair, it's almost connected to Chapala, with a population approaching 55,000.

The climate, at an elevation of 1,500 m (5,000 ft) above sea level, is moderate. Much like other locations in the Sierra Madre, the average highs are mid- to upper-20s °C (75–80°F) and the temperature only reaches 30°C (90°F) on occasional days in April and May. Due to the elevation, lows will hit 5–6°C (low-40s °F) in January and February overnight, but temperatures will warm up during the day.

The rainy season runs May to October with most rainfall occurring in July and August. Humidity is low in the winters, below 40%, but reaching 80% and higher in the rainy season. We all love water views, but with water comes humidity. It's science.

Miguel Hidalgo y Costilla Guadalajara International Airport (GDL) is conveniently located about halfway to Ajijic and Lake Chapala from Guadalajara. It's one of the nicest, and easiest, airports I have been in. Not too big and well-organized. It handles nearly 13 million passengers a year, ranking third busiest behind Mexico City and Cancún.

While it has direct flights to most major American cities, Canada- or Europe-bound passengers will need to connect via a short flight to Mexico City.

The population of the Chapala municipality (including Ajijic) is about 60,000, swelling over the winter months with the influx of snowbirds, as noted previously. In the summer months, you do get some 'sunbirds'—those escaping the summer heat and humidity in the southern US.

If you're looking for more authentic Mexican (and almost a beach town feel), you should have a look at Chapala proper. The malecón (boardwalk) is small, but growing, and attracts a number of vendors on weekends and weekdays during the season.

Ajijic is a gorgeous colonial town with cobblestone streets (all of them), upscale boutiques and sophisticated restaurants. Living in the Centro in Ajijic can be challenging for noise, as there are a lot of fiestas and fireworks throughout the year. There are many weekend homes in Ajijic and residents of Guadalajara (called Tapatíos) have long had places on the lake. It is a quaint, pretty town.

For box stores (other than Walmart in Ajijic), head to Guadalajara. Everything can be found there. Plus, there are local markets—the Ajijic's open air tianguis is on Wednesdays and the organic market is on Tuesdays in the west end of town. The open air market in Chapala is on Mondays. There is a grocery store that has been in Ajijic forever called Super Lake that imports hard-to-find gringo items (at a premium) and there is a large Soriana supermarket in Chapala.

There are great folk art boutiques in Ajijic and the malecón (boardwalk) at Chapala has some vendors, mostly on weekends when the lake shore is filled with weekenders. There are annual folk art and indigenous art festivals that attract incredible artists from all around Mexico.

There are a small number of good private and public hospitals in Ajijic/Chapala but some of the best medical care in the country is less than an hour away in Guadalajara.

The Ajijic area has some wonderful old colonial homes and great lake views. The climate is superb and you won't have to speak Spanish to live here, although—as is the case in Mexico in general—you will get much more out of the experience if you do. There's a highly organized and large gringo community, probably one of the largest in all of Mexico. Everything you want and access to an international airport is less than an hour away. And if you buy a home and change your mind later, this is one of the most liquid real estate markets in Mexico (along with San Miguel, Puerto Vallarta and Cancún).

Morelia, Michoacán

Evidence of human settlement in the area goes back to the 6th century and the indigenous Purépecha, who were based around nearby Lake Pátzcuaro, dominated in the pre-Hispanic period. In the 1520s, the Spanish took control of the area.

Morelia's Purépecha name was Uaianarhio and you will still hear this spoken today—along with many nicknames such as *The Garden of New Spain*, *City of Pink Stone* and *City of Open Doors*. It was renamed Morelia in 1828, in honor of José María Morelos y Pavón, a Mexican priest and rebel leader who helped organize the War of Independence. Morelos is a national hero in Mexico. The city of Morelia played a major role in the Mexican War of Independence movement and is truly a historic location.

Morelia was declared a UNESCO World Heritage Site in 1991, recognized for its outstanding colonial buildings and town square design, as well as its historical significance.

Morelia is located just over 300 km (185 mi) almost due east of Mexico City. Elevation is 1,900 m (6,200 ft) above sea level.

A subtropical highland climate, the average highs are mid- to upper-20s °C (75–80°F) year-round and the temperature only reaches 30°C (90°F) on occasional days in April and May. Due to the elevation, lows will hit 5–6°C (low-40s °F) in January and February overnight, but warm up during the day. You will need some form of heating for the winter nights as the masonry houses hold the cold in their bones.

Rainy season is May to October with July seeing the most rain. Humidity is well below 50% most of the year, except in the height of the rainy season (primarily in July) when it spikes to 65%. With the exception of the colder nights in January and February (when you can head to the beach), Morelia has a very agreeable climate.

You will have to learn some Spanish, but it's not that bad, now, is it? You'll be hard pressed to find a menu in English—or any English, really—except at the tourist sites. And there are some good language schools in Morelia. While there is a definite expat population, it's not overt and they don't live in specific areas. The expats here are sprinkled around town.

Morelia is a three-hour drive from Mexico City. General Francisco Mujica International Airport (MLM), known simply as Morelia

International Airport, serves more than 1.4 million passengers a year and offers direct flights to many US cities, including San Francisco, Chicago and most of the US South. At this time, there are no direct flights to Canada, but a connecting flight via Mexico City provides a plethora of choices in 50 minutes' travel time—and buses to the Mexico City airport are also available.

The population of Morelia is just under a million, making it a bona fide city. As noted, there is a significant expat population, but it is certainly not in your face and, in a city this size, blends in easily with the local population. More of an integrated city than you find in smaller, gringo-dominated towns like Ajijic and San Miguel.

Expats are everywhere but the more preferred neighborhoods tend to be in the Centro, with old colonial buildings and lots of history. If you choose to live outside the periférico (the ring-road around the city), Santa María de Guido is a good choice. With Morelia's size, you'll find all the box stores—Costco, Sam's and Walmart. And of course, local markets, supermarkets and department stores. There's a wonderful artisan market and even a Nike outlet store. You won't be lacking shopping opportunities in Morelia.

Morelia's public hospitals include Hospital General and IMSS HGZ 83. Private hospitals include Hospital Memorial and FEMEDI.

As yet, relatively undiscovered by the masses, Morelia has a reasonable climate and all the conveniences one might imagine in city this size. In addition, it has rich history and incredible colonial architecture. There is an expat community, but they assimilate and don't constitute an economic ratio that begins to change things. All in all, a decent place to live if you don't mind a commuter flight to Mexico City, or having a few cold nights in the winter. A simple solution if you own your home is to install a gas fireplace in your bedroom with a remote control. When you wake up, flip it on for half an hour and all is well.

Pátzcuaro, Michoacán

The Chimichecas settled the Pátzcuaro area in the 1320s, a nomadic hunter-gatherer tribe that roamed the northern valley of Mexico. The Spanish made relatively quick work of them in 1526. In 1538, the Spanish re-established their settlement of Pátzcuaro and made it the capital of the new Spanish state.

It was during the presidency of Lázaro Cárdenas (1934–40) that it became a tourism hub and cultural destination (he was from Michoacán). And while it is a very popular domestic tourist destination year-round, it is the town's Día de Muertos (Day of the Dead) celebrations that attract tourists from around the world. It is one of the best places in all of Mexico to observe this holiday, where an illuminated Noche de Muertos (Night of the Dead) is celebrated around the lake.

Located on Lake Pátzcuaro, the town is approximately 350 km (220 mi) almost due west (as the crow files) from Mexico City. It's about a 45-minute drive from Morelia, the state capital, and a four-hour drive from either Guadalajara or Mexico City.

This is authentic Mexico. It is the market hub of the region, where artisans bring their specialized crafts, such as black pottery, baskets and copper goods. Most of the streets in the Centro are cobblestone and trailing flowers drip from Juliet balconies down to the street.

At 2,140 m (7,000 ft) above sea level, you will go down to single digits Celsius (40s °F) overnight in January and February. But the daytime highs are 20–25°C in the winter (70–80°F) with lots of sun. Summer weather will hit 30°C (90°F) in May with lows of 10–15°C (50–60°F). It's a very moderate climate.

The rainy season runs from June to September with the wettest month being July. Humidity normally runs around 60%, spiking to 80% in the worst of the rainy season. But, with such moderate temperatures, the humidity isn't much of an issue.

You'll have to speak Spanish to live in this town. It is authentic Mexico and there aren't a lot of international tourists, except for Day of the Dead. So maybe for two days, when the tour companies are in town, you can speak English. It's a small town as well, but Morelia, with a decent expat population, is only 60 km (40 mi) away if you're in need of some expat services.

Being only 45 minutes away—Morelia is the logical airport to use. Morelia International Airport (MLM) serves more than 1.4 million passengers a year and offers direct flights to many US cities, including San Francisco, Chicago and most of the US South. To reach Canada or Europe, you'll have to connect via Mexico City, but flights are frequent, short and inexpensive.

The population of Pátzcuaro is around 100,000—a decent size for finding local services like supermarkets, local fresh markets and tiendas specializing in most everything. For other purchases, Morelia is close by.

The public hospitals here are Clínica Hospital ISSSTE and Hospital General Dr Gabriel García. There are private hospitals, such as Clínica San José Pátzcuaro. With Morelia so close, any serious conditions should be attended there.

Pátzcuaro is a visually pleasing town. It is a small town in a bit of an out-of-the-way location and there is an even smaller expat community, but bound to grow. There are many artists, writers and sculptors who come for the tranquility and setting. The fact that it can be a little colder—and Spanish is a requirement—does keep out the type of expat who wants to live in a more Americanized setting.

Pátzcuaro is charming, though, and Morelia is within striking distance if this kind of peaceful Mexican life is on your bucket list.

Chapter 8:

Colonial highlands south

Mexico City, Cuernavaca, Puebla, Taxco, Oaxaca, San Cristóbal

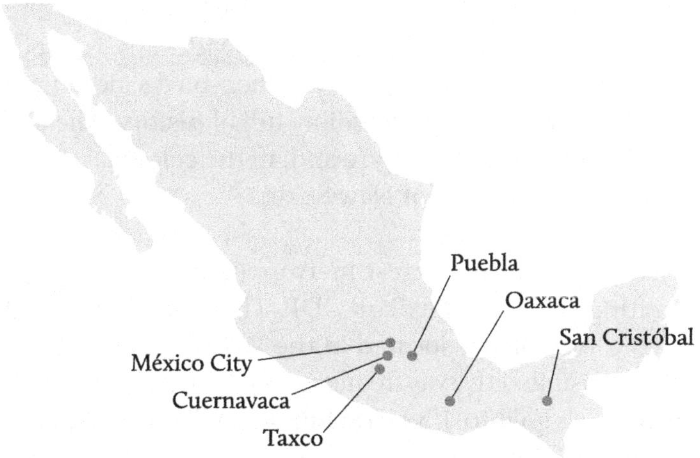

History just oozes from all the colonial highlands. Everything from the Aztec canals of Xochimilco in Mexico City to the cathedrals of San Cristóbal will enchant the history buff. You're moving south and, for the most part, these towns are warming up, but still have moderate climates due to elevation. The big exception is San Cristóbal—while the furthest south of the group, it sees the lowest temperatures overnight in winter, sitting at 2,200 m (7,200 ft) above sea level.

The land changes from arid to temperate around Mexico City (think desert to subtropical), so the flora and fauna are different than north of the country's capital. It's also warmer in most locations, with nighttime lows rarely dipping below 15°C (60°F).

The cuisine is still pork-based but you'll see much more queso Oaxaca (a Oaxacan white, mozzarella-type cheese) and a few more delicacies like blue corn tortillas, chapulínes and escamoles due to indigenous influences in food—see *Chapter 20: A gringo primer on food in Mexico.*

Mexico City

Mexico City, or Mexico as it is known to Mexicans, is impossible to describe. You need to go there, whether you decide to live there or not. It's immense and incredibly full of history. The city was the capital of the Aztec empire and, in the colonial era, Mexico City became the capital of New Spain.

Mexico City is of the largest metropolitan cities in the world, generating 15.8% of Mexico's GDP. There are 16 boroughs in Mexico City, which is located in the Valle de Mexico (Valley of Mexico). Seismic activity is frequent and there are water problems that we won't go into. If you're thinking of living here, you need to do some serious research, but we consider it one of the best places in all of Mexico to live.

The climate is subtropical highland, mitigated by elevation. It's warmer than the colonial cities to the north by a few degrees but can get cool in the winter—occasionally single digits Celsius (40s °F) on the coldest nights—and can be muggy in the rainy season. Its elevation, at 2,240 m (7,350 ft) above sea level can be hard on people with breathing difficulties.

The rainy season is June to October, with concentrated rains in the summer months. Torrential, warm rain usually comes in the (late) afternoons. If you're caught at lunch and it starts to rain, that means it is time for an afternoon *tarde tequilera*—when you have no choice but to sit under the covered patio and sip tequila until it's over.

You probably don't have to speak a lot of Spanish, as most of the people in Mexico City speak two languages. But speaking Spanish is courteous, and it's the language of choice for Mexicans. Two good reasons to learn.

The Mexico City International Airport (MEX)—officially Benito Juárez International Airport—rocks. It's a busy airport, but it's not often crowded. There are direct flights to the US, Europe and Canada at multiple times during the day.

The population of Mexico City is 9.2 million but greater Mexico City is 22 million. Yet, it is only the 23rd most populous city in the world. It is, however, the most populous city in the Americas.

Mexico City has more museums than any other city in the world—well over 100—and many of them are major, world-class museums. And art galleries. Too many to mention. The historical Centro with its zócalo (main square) is an incredible experience.

The best places to live, we think, are Roma and Condesa. Polanco is nice too, and very upscale. A lot more expensive. San Ángel is a great neighborhood (read: old money). And Santa Fe has modern buildings and many of the working expats live in this area, being the business center of the city. We lived in Mexico City for a short period.

Having dogs, we had to have substantial outdoor space, so we rented in the south end of the city. It really wasn't the Mexico City experience we were looking for. But the cool neighborhoods, like Roma and Condesa, are very expensive when you need a house with a yard. They are full of wonderful converted lofts and mansions with killer suites at rates that are starting to climb, but still cheaper than cities like Vancouver or New York. But houses are few and far between—it's that old supply and demand thing.

Mexico City has every box store in the world, including some you've never heard of. I can't even begin to count the Costcos and City Markets. Astounding. There is nothing you can't find—even IKEA.

We can't even begin to name the number of public Hospital Generals or IMSS or ISSSTE hospitals in Mexico City. Ditto private hospitals—they are all over the city, although concentrated in Tlalpan, a suburb in the south of the city. These are world class hospitals.

And, oh boy, if you are a city lover, this is the place you want to be, I kid you not. It's not cheap. But it's not the most expensive place in the world to live. The most expensive in Mexico? Probably. But worth every penny. Do your research. Rent for one or two months maximum—a place to land while you check out all the neighborhoods. Better yet, try to visit a few times. It's a big city. A really big city. If that's not your thing, you do not want to live here (you can always visit).

Cuernavaca

The first Aztec emperor expanded his conquests to this area in 1370, although remains have been found in the state dating to 1000 BC. The Spanish invaded the area in the 1520s, Cortés constructed his castle in Cuernavaca in 1526. Morelos was imprisoned in that castle during the Mexican War of Independence.

Maximilian and his wife Carlota had a weekend home in *The City of Eternal Spring* when he was installed as Emperor of Mexico in Mexico City. The last Shah of Iran (Mohammad Reza Pahlavi) came to Cuernavaca in exile, as did Mama Doc (Simone Duvalier) whose husband and son were Haitian dictators. The houses were next door to each other and I've been in the Duvalier house. Apparently, former US Secretary of State Henry Kissinger met with the Shah and Baby Doc in the ornate dining room for dinner on numerous occasions. One can only imagine.

Many Hollywood writers and directors came in self-imposed exile during the Joseph McCarthy years, and it was said to be popular among retired CIA agents. Emperor of Ethiopia Haile Selassie and actor Gary Cooper had vacation homes here. Woolworth heiress Barbara Hutton built an estate in the south end of town and actress Rita Hayworth had a residence in town, as did actress Helen Hayes.

The elite of Mexico City have always had weekend homes here—the weather is a good 10°C warmer in the winter and cooler in the summer than even Mexico City. We're on the south side of the mountain and that makes a huge difference—I live here so you're getting first-hand information.

It's an interesting city—most of her beauty is behind her walls. It takes a while to grow fond of her but the climate is the first thing that I loved. Cuernavaca has more swimming pools per capita than any city in the world, with the exception of Beverly Hills.

Lows of 12°C (55°F) in the worst of the winter and in the 15–18°C range (60–67°F) during summer. Highs year round are consistently 27–28°C (80–82°F). Rainy season runs May to September, with September being the wettest month. Generally, it rains in the evening or overnight—big tropical thunderstorms. Humidity runs in the mid-30% range in the winter and up to the mid-50% range in the rainy season. It does depend on where you live in Cuernavaca.

Cuernavaca has a range of micro-climates thanks to her barrancas (canyons). There are a series of barrancas, 50+ m (165+ ft) deep running north to south throughout the city, referred to as the 'lungs of Cuernavaca'. Also, the city is positioned on a steep, south-facing mountain. There is more than 1,000 m (3,300 ft) difference in elevation from the north to the south and, as a result, the south has considerably more heat and humidity in the summer. And will be less cool in the winter. I have a friend who lives just 1 km away (she's south of me) and, noticing that some of her orchids bloomed much earlier than mine, we checked the difference in altitude—more than 300 m (1,000 ft) in 1 km.

There is an expat community, many of whom have been in Cuernavaca for decades. It's not large compared to the size of the city (municipality is nearly a million and city proper is about 400,000). Estimates are less than 2,000 expats but there are email and Facebook groups. You really do need to speak Spanish. While there is a large, educated middle class who speak English as well as Spanish, the service and retail industries all operate in Spanish. But you're in luck—at last count there were more than 50 Spanish schools in Cuernavaca, making it the largest concentration of Spanish language schools outside Seville, Spain.

Cuernavaca does have an airport but there are no commercial flights (there were commuter flights at one time)—just private planes. The Mexico City airport (MEX) is about two hours away by direct bus (depending on the traffic and at which terminal you are getting off) and they leave every 40 minutes. The Mexico City airport, of course, has direct flights pretty much everywhere.

There is a large middle class in Cuernavaca and plenty of different neighborhoods to choose from. There really isn't a bad neighborhood, but some are poorer than others and this is pretty evident from visual clues. As always, get yourself a good real estate agent with local knowledge, even when renting.

That said, here's the lowdown. The north of town is cooler and less humid than the south of town. We're talking up to 10°C (20°F) difference and double-digit humidity differences, so don't discount this info. Mid-town are the San Diego and Vista Hermosa areas—probably the most popular upper-middle class neighborhoods (and the trendiest). The really high-end 'hood is Palmira, in the south of town, and its hot. It's the old money (insanely wealthy, in many cases) part of town. There are many neighborhoods in the north that are desirable—and anything on a barranca has a killer view.

All the box stores are here—Costco, Sam's, Walmart, Home Depot. And the normal Mexican supermarkets and department stores—Mega, Soriana, La Comer, Fresko and City Market. There's Liverpool, Bed, Bath & Beyond, PetCo—and US food chains like IHOP, Carlos'n Charlie's, Chili's Grill & Bar. The only one I've been to is P F Chang's.

Aside from the big malls and box stores, the main public market is huge—everything from hanging pigs' heads to religious candles. It can almost be overwhelming. Mercado Lomas de la Selva, north of the Centro, is more manageable and has the same offerings, if not the variety. Depends on what you're looking for—the incredible visuals of a huge central market, or a fast trip to pick up a few oranges and limes.

For public healthcare, Hospital General Dr José G Parres gets good marks. Private hospitals, such as Sanatorio Henri Dunant and Instituto Mexicano de Trasplantes are popular choices. For specialty care, you are close to Mexico City.

In summary, I live here so this is not really an objective summary (at least I'm honest). The climate is great and there are big US-style stores, as well as a variety of Mexican markets and small tiendas. There is a gringo community. They are assimilated and you need to find them but start on the internet and Facebook.

The cost of living is lower than Mexico City but you're only an hour-and-a-half to two hours away, not just from the airport but from one of the most dynamic cities in the world. Cuernavaca herself is a walled city and her beauty is behind those walls.

I'll never forget the first time I saw Cuernavaca—on a day tour from Mexico City. We'd already extensively explored Mexico City, Ajijic and San Miguel—all of which have incredible architecture and are beautiful cities, visually. Well, an aside, one of my Mexican friends always says I'm not actually talking about Mexico City when I say Mexico City. I'm talking about specific parts of Mexico City—Roma, Condesa, Polanco. She's right. But I digress.

There are some pretty cities in colonial Mexico. I had been told how beautiful Cuernavaca is. When the tour bus pulled into town, I was really shocked. And disappointed. Because on the outside, I think she's kind of ugly. But inside—that's the pearl in the oyster. Once you get behind a few walls (start at the restaurant, Las Mañanitas)—you'll understand.

Taxco, Guerrero

In pre-Hispanic times, the Taxco region was an extremely important place as the seat of an Aztec governor. Taxco was one of the first mining centers to be inhabited by the Spaniards. And, while the silver has been pretty much mined out, the town today enjoys a brisk trade in silver jewelry and other silver pieces.

The Taxco silver designers are probably the most famous in the world, beginning in a very unlikely way—with an expat. William Spratling, a New Yorker, came to Taxco in the 1920s and revived the silver industry in Taxco.

The silver jewelry trade boomed during the second World War when luxury items from Europe were no longer available in the USA. And, by 1945, his silver workshop employed more than 400 people and he was the darling of the town, with commercial silver mining already on the downturn.

Major stores like Tiffany & Co, Neiman Marcus and Saks Fifth Avenue sold Taxco designer silver. And people like the Rockefellers, Marilyn Monroe and George Gershwin made it a trendy place to visit.

Today, thanks to Spratling—and Margot de Taxco, Antonio Castillo, Antonio Piñeda, Hector Aguilar et al—putting Taxco on the map, there are still thousands of working silversmiths in the region today.

Taxco is one of the prettiest colonial towns in all of Mexico, the houses are white with red tile roofs—very Spanish in style. The streets are steep, windy and paved with dark cobblestones. It is located just 160 km (100 mi) southwest of Mexico City.

Taxco's climate is one of the most consistent year-round climates in Mexico. Highs run 25–28°C (77–83°F) and lows are consistently 16–18°C (60s °F). It sites at 1,700 m (5,600 ft) above sea level. Rainy season runs May to October and the humidity will top 75% in June and July but, with moderate temperatures, it's not such an issue.

This is a Spanish-speaking town but also a big tourist town—being a short trip from Mexico City, it is on many tours. The tourists are mostly around the main square and the few surrounding blocks and, in some of the stores, you will find English spoken. Certainly in the silver shops. But it's a Mexican town.

Mexico City is only 100 km (60 mi) away and there is a bus that will not deliver you to the airport, but to the Metro Tasqueña station, from which you can get an authorized cab or Uber to Mexico City airport. It's a bit of a pain. The drive would probably be close to three hours.

The population is about 100,000 now and there is a Walmart, but you'll have to make the trip north to Cuernavaca—50 km (30 mi)—to do any Home Depot, Sam's Club or Costco shopping. But with 60,000 people, you have all the Mexican supermarkets you need and their local farmers' market is always getting fantastic reviews.

And just as a point of interest—the poinsettia (known in Mexico as the *flor de Noche Buena*, the Christmas Eve flower)—was discovered in the fields of Taxco by US ambassador Joel Poinsett in 1820s and it enchanted him. He sent it home to Charleston SC one Christmas and the rest is history.

The IMSS Hospital General is the largest public hospital and there are good small clinics such as Hospital Ángeles—both

Cuernavaca and Mexico City are close by in case of a more complicated diagnosis.

In summary, it's a small town and it's the steepest town I have ever been to in Mexico (and I've lived up the hill in San Miguel). Very narrow, windy streets, cobblestones, next to impossible to drive in the Centro—which is why everyone, including cabbies, drive Volkswagen Beetles. But it's one of the prettiest towns in Mexico with not bad access to the Mexico City airport (MEX) and a superb climate. But it is small, and there are not many expats. If you can navigate steep hills, are happy to learn Spanish and small-town living is for you—you may have met your match in Taxco.

A note on the state of Guerrero—it's one of Mexico's poorest and most violent states. While Taxco is in the northwest of the state and not itself a dangerous place, you do not want to find yourself on some back mountain road in the state of Guerrero. I don't mean to scare people off—if you want to live in Taxco it is not a dangerous place to live. But you really need to be hyper aware of the region you are living in and plan to travel on toll roads. Taxco is very close to the toll road and you can get anywhere from there.

Puebla, Puebla

The city was founded in 1531 as a Spanish city—one of the few locations not founded on the former site of a pre-Columbian settlement. The area, according to historians, had no real pre-Columbian history, only being used in the early 1500s as a site for warring tribes to duke it out.

Still, it was a very important Spanish city. Famous for its architecture, from Renaissance to Mexican Baroque, the city was named a UNESCO World Heritage Site in 1987. The city is also famous for mole poblano, chiles en nogada (the national dish, served everywhere during independence month of September but served here year-round) and Talavera pottery. Between 1550 and 1570, Spanish potters from Talavera de la Reina in Spain came to Puebla to teach the locals how to master this art form. Puebla is world-renowned for this technique to this day.

It was an important city, midway between the main port (Veracruz) and the capital, and remains important today. It's located about 100 km (60 mi) southeast of Mexico City. The Battle of Puebla, where the Mexicans defeated the French, happened here on May 5—which is where the Americans get their Cinco de Mayo celebration (which is not widely celebrated in Mexico).

There is still some commercial farming but 80% of the city's economy today is based on industry. The main employers are HYLSA, who manufacture and export galvanized steel products, and Volkswagen who have an automotive plant in Puebla.

The climate is subtropical highland and the temperatures are mitigated by the elevation of 2,135 m (7,000 ft). Popocatépetl, the volcano and second highest peak in Mexico, is close by and stands at 5,426 m (17,800 ft). These are mountains. In the winter, the middle of the night temperatures will hit single digits (about 40°F), due to the altitude. But in the day, it will be sunny and in the low- to mid-20s °C (75–80°F). In the summer, lows seldom go below 10°C (50°F) and highs will range from 25–28°C (80–85°F). It's a very consistent climate.

Rainy season runs May to September, with June to August being the wettest months. Humidity ranges from 50–60% most of the year.

This is a Mexican city. You need to speak Spanish. No ifs, ands or buts. There is a large middle class and many people do speak English as a second language, but most of the service industry is Spanish only.

There are well over 3 million people in Puebla and, despite having a well-preserved and very historic Centro, this is a modern city with all the accouterments.

Puebla International Airport (PBC), officially known as Hermanos Serdán International Airport, offers direct flights to Houston (United), but there are numerous daily flights and shuttles to the

Mexico City airport. Canadians and Europeans can catch nonstop flights in Mexico City. A new, larger terminal pushed passenger traffic up in recent years to just under 1 million passengers annually, including direct flights from Houston TX.

Although it's Mexico's fourth largest city, Puebla has not attracted a lot of US expats, as it's further from the border than most, and not a tourist town, per se. However, there is a steady stream of European expats (German, primarily), who come to Puebla to work in the automotive industry. There are expat neighborhoods in Puebla. One is Chipilo, an Italian neighborhood, and another is San Rafael, a French neighborhood. Puebla also has a number of Lebanese expats and large number of Spanish expats.

There are box stores galore—Costco, Sam's, three Walmarts, Home Depot, even IHOP, Applebee's and Pizza Hut. All the traditional Mexican local markets, supermarkets and department stores as well. Once you are in a Mexican city that is approaching a million people (and this one is over three), you have every convenience at your fingertips.

Public hospitals include the Hospitals General—one in the north and one in the south—and the IMSS Specialty Hospital. Among the many private hospitals are the Puebla branches of Hospital Ángeles and Hospital MAC.

In summary—Puebla is a pretty city (I've been there for chiles en nogada and Talavera pottery) with a historic Centro and a pleasing vibe. It's a big city full of all the big city pleasures—car dealerships, shopping malls and bypasses. But it is a very clean and very attractive place, even in the industrial areas. Kind of like the southern version of Querétaro. If you can handle temperatures of 10°C (50°F) overnight in January and February, and connecting flights, you'll love this vibrant city.

Oaxaca, Oaxaca

The Aztecs entered the Oaxaca Valley in 1440, but the city was founded in 1529 by a small group of Zapotecs. After the Independence of Mexico in 1821, the city became the seat of the municipality, and today both city and state are named Oaxaca. Kind of confusing—but assume we are talking about the city unless we specify it is the state. Tourism was developed in the 1980s based on the two largest assets of the state—indigenous art and mezcal (more on that later). And the city became the obvious distribution hub for both.

In 1994, the Mexico City–Oaxaca highway was completed and provided a much-needed, quick transportation corridor. The violent 2006 Oaxaca protests (which began as teachers' strike) quelled tourism for a few years but it has rebounded and continues to do so. In the last 25 years, tourism has become a major economic factor for Oaxaca and more than 77% of the city's employment is related to tourism.

Small wonder. It is a cultural mecca, especially for indigenous art—18 different indigenous groups retain their own languages and traditions statewide. There are entire towns within day trips of Oaxaca dedicated to the creation of alebrijes (brightly colored, carved mythical creatures), barro negro pottery (Doña Rosa, in particular), hand-woven blankets and rugs made traditionally with natural dyes like wild marigold, green glazed pottery, huipiles (embroidered tunics) and much more. Add to that gastronomic delights such as grasshopper tacos (seriously), chocolate to die for, and the recently trending mezcal liquors.

There are many local markets where you can find these treasures, including the Artisan market, where folk art from around the state is sold. Lots of history, too. Lots of museums and churches. El Árbol del Tule, the Tree of Tule, estimated to be around 1,600 years old, is in the town center. Monte Albán, all of 4 km from Oaxaca, was the first great city of Mesoamerica. It is estimated to have been established in 500 BC. All in all, a fair bit to keep you busy for some time if you are a learner.

We would be remiss if we didn't say a bit more about mezcal—the 'tequila' of Oaxaca. Another appellation regulated product, it is recognized internationally as coming from only specific regions and manufacturers. Mezcal can be made from one of 28 different types of agave (but tequila can only use one type, the blue agave). The process is different than that of tequila and the taste is smoky.

Oaxaca city sits in the middle of Oaxaca state, 450 km (280 mi) southeast of Mexico City. It's about 250 km (155 mi) to Puerto Escondido on the Pacific coast. But at 1,550 m (5,000 ft) above sea level in the Sierra Madre, the climate is much more moderate than the coast.

Oaxaca weather is noted for its mild, spring-like climate, much like Cuernavaca. Highs rarely exceed 30°C (90°F) and stay consistently above 10°C (50°F) overnight during the coldest points in winter. Humidity ranges from the low-50% range to the upper-60% range. Rainy season is May to September with gentle rains generally falling later in the day.

You'll need some Spanish if you plan to live here. And maybe more—7–8% of residents speak one of the 18 indigenous languages. English is not widely spoken, as many of the tourists are domestic, although you will find English menus in the main areas. This is a city for gringos who want to explore Mexican culture and assimilate, not for gringos who want to live like they did up north. There are language schools in Oaxaca—and many online and app options—for learning another language.

Just 7 km south of the city, Xoxocotlán International Airport (OAX) handles almost 1.7 million passengers a year. Many international visitors land in Mexico City and catch connecting flights on Mexican airlines, but American offers direct flights to Dallas/Fort Worth and United to Houston. And there are many direct flights from other locations inside Mexico. The flights to and from Mexico City take just 1 hour 15 minutes, and are inexpensive and frequent. Once you are in Mexico City, the world is your oyster as far as flight choices.

With a population just over 700,000, the city offers a variety of choices as far as where to live. Xochimilco, La Cascada and Reforma are all reasonable residential neighborhoods close to the Centro. And then there is the Centro itself, full of historic old buildings. The further out you go from the Centro, the better your Spanish should be. Many expats choose Oaxaca for its culture, art and colonial history, so learning the language is a no-brainer for them.

It's one of those pretty Mexican cities and a UNESCO World Heritage Site. There is an expat community, but that's not why anyone moves there. It's more about the culture. There is a Sam's Club, but no Costco. Many of your food purchases will be from local and organic markets but major Mexican supermercados and department stores have a presence in the city.

Public hospital options include Hospital General Dr Aurelio Valdivieso and IMSS Hospital General Zone 1. Private hospitals are plentiful in a city this size, and two of the highest rated are Clínica Hospital de Urgencias Médicas and Hospital San Antonio.

In summary—near perfect weather with a lot of culture and history in a city large enough to supply most of your needs (and Mexico City just a short plane ride, or drive, away). While a very safe place to live, it is one of the most marginalized states in all of Mexico and Oaxaca is the state capital—so there are lots of protests. Sometimes they shut down highways for days. But overall, an interesting and charming place to seep yourself in Mexico and her culture.

San Cristóbal (de las Casas), Chiapas

We've come a long way south to the southernmost state in Mexico—900 km southwest of Mexico City to be exact (about 500 mi), as the crow flies. Founded by the Spanish in 1528, San Cristóbal is just 150 km (90 mi) north of Guatemala, sitting on the central plains of the Chiapas highlands. In pre-Hispanic times it was inhabited by the Tzotzil and the Tzatzal people, and the area today contains one of the largest indigenous Mayan populations in Mexico. The town is set in a highland valley surrounded by forest and is truly a mountain town.

Designated a *Pueblo Mágico*, San Cris (as the town is referred to) is perhaps one of the most romantic colonial cities in Mexico. It's certainly getting a reputation as one of the coolest colonial cities. Narrow cobblestone streets, homes painted in bright colors, and little shops and tiendas retain the town's Spanish-colonial charm. There was a Zapatista uprising in 1994, which you will hear much about, but the town has returned to the tranquil mountain paradise it always was. You'll find that Zapatista merchandise—tee shirts and dolls—still sell well in the central markets.

At 2,200 m (7,200 ft) above sea level, it's cold at night. The temperature drops to upper single digits (low-40s °F) overnight from late October to April. That said, it will go below freezing (0°C or 32°F) on occasion in January and February. You need to be prepared for that, despite being so far south.

And there is no central heating in Mexico, remember? However, you can install gas fireplaces—we installed two in our San Miguel house—one in the main social zone (which was an open layout) and one in our bedroom. With remotes. Worked like a charm and they looked great. They heat the rooms inside of an hour once you wake up and, by then, the sun is doing the heating.

It never gets too warm in San Cris. The highs, in the warmest months of April and May, will hit 25°C (80°F). Rainy season runs from May to October but humidity is consistently around 80% and fog is common on winter mornings. It can be muggy at times, despite the low temperatures.

You need to learn Spanish to live in this city, we're almost on top of the Guatemalan border. And Spanish won't help with the portion of the population that speaks an indigenous language. There are four or five language schools in San Cris and lots of learning available online. You don't have to be fluent. But you do have to be able to live comfortably and master day-to-day transactions and chores. You really won't get much out of living in this town if you don't speak the language.

The closest commercial airport is just an hour away, with plenty of shuttle services. Tuxtla Gutierrez International Airport (TGZ), officially Ángel Albino Corzo International Airport, handles almost 1.8 million passengers a year. There are no nonstop international flights to the US or Canada, but connecting flights to Mexico City are frequent and inexpensive.

The San Cris population is almost 200,000 and there is an expat community, but it is not large relative to the size of the town. They're opening international restaurants in the Centro—Chinese, Middle Eastern, French—even vegetarian. It's a popular tourist destination for Mexicans and Europeans, but somewhat undiscovered by Americans—although that may be changing. Nonstop flights matter a lot where tourism is concerned.

The town is large enough for a Sam's Club, and there's a Walmart on the highway some distance out of town. But between the supermarkets (Soriana, Chedraui, Mega) and the local produce and meat markets, this town has everything you need.

San Cris is famous for its art and textile markets—and its weaving, embroidery and folk art. The artisan markets are spectacular and full of bargains. Chiapas is one of the poorest Mexican states and the indigenous artists bring their handmade treasures to San Cris to sell.

Public hospitals include ISSSTE-Clínica Hospital San Cristóbal de las Casas and Hospital de Las Culturas. This city has very highly rated private hospitals, including Hospital Colonial and San Cristóbal Medical Center.

In summary—lots going on and if you like a cooler night for sleeping, this is your town. The temperatures are great for sleeping, just not so great for getting up at 6am. There is an active arts community and several music venues—a fair bit to keep you busy.

It's certainly off the beaten path and, for some, a little cold. You'll have to learn Spanish and getting in and out of the country is a bit more effort than some places, but it all depends on what you want from the place you live in.

Chapter 9:

The next step

You've figured out where you want to go. Now, what do you need to begin your journey?

You'll need a visa.

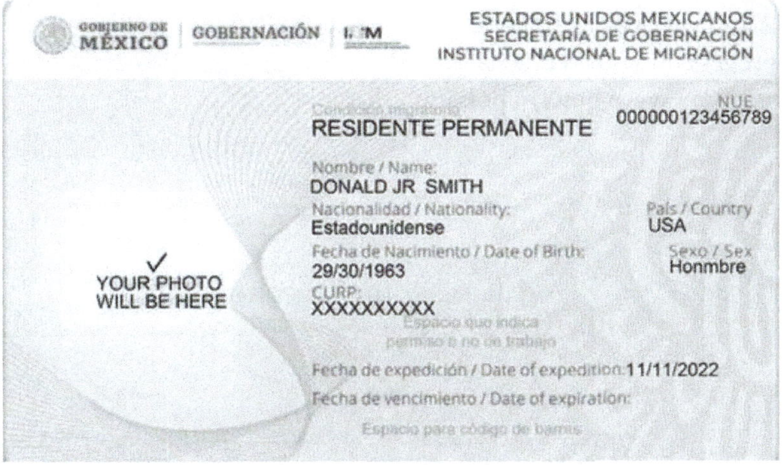

Now that you have an idea of the general area where you'd like to live, you need to figure out how to do it. Tourist visas are issued at the airport when you land or when you cross the border as tourist/visitor. They can be issued for up to 180 days but, lately, they have been issued for far shorter times at many entry points. In this book we will deal only with the visas that allow you to live in Mexico full time.

If you're sure you want to stay in Mexico forever, then go ahead and apply for a permanent residence visa (and possibly even citizenship in the future). If you're more like we were, and think you'd better try it for a few years first, then go for the temporary resident visa.

A temporary resident visa is usually issued for a one-year period initially and, before this expires, you may choose to renew it for another one, two or three years. After being in the country on a temporary resident visa for four years, you are automatically entitled to permanent resident status, but you do need to submit the paperwork in a limited time-frame, so pay attention.

If you choose not to go to permanent status, you must begin the process for your temporary resident permit from the beginning—as if you were newly applying.

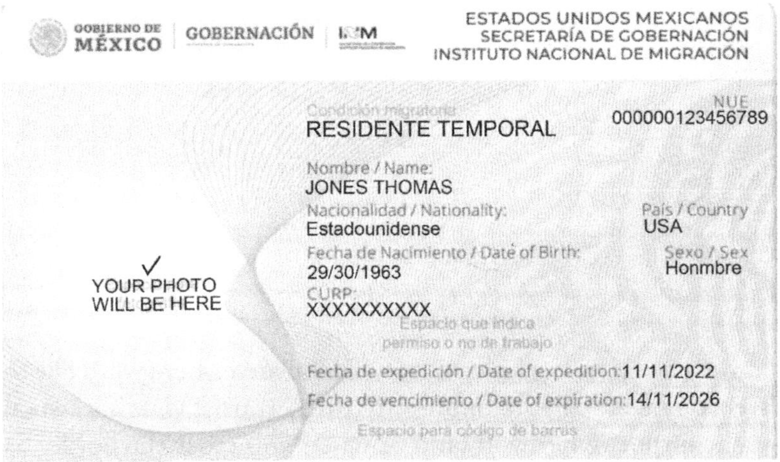

And herein lies the rub. Since 2013, all temporary and permanent resident visas must be pre-approved by the consulate closest to your home. At least, that's what they say—although I have heard that the border towns closest to Mexico, such as Laredo and San

Diego, will process visas from out-of-state and from Canada. It's usually easier to process from your home consulate but, in any event, you must begin the process outside Mexico. With few exceptions (and I will deal with those), you cannot obtain a visa from inside the country.

Once you apply for a visa and are approved, your consulate will issue an approval and adhere a holographic visa in your passport. At this point, you must activate this approval by crossing the border (whether entry is by car or plane) within six months of its issuance.

Ayudita: Once your visa is issued—do not leave the consulate without first checking your pre-approved visa in your passport. Make sure your name is spelled correctly and any details are accurate. If you applied as a temporary resident but were issued a permanent resident pre-approval in error, your car will be illegal after 30 days. This does happen. There is more information in *Chapter 11: Transportation.*

Once you do cross the border, you will only have 30 days in which to begin the process so you need to tend to this immediately upon arrival.

If you enter Mexico at an airport which has passport scanners, as a temporary or permanent resident you **must not** go through the automatic scanners. They are meant for tourists. Should you do so, you will be a classified as a tourist and you will need to start the process over again at the consulate.

What qualifies me for residency?

Mostly money. You need more money to go straight to permanent resident, less to qualify as a legal temporary resident of up to four years. After that, you can move to permanent residency without showing any further financial records. The amount of income and/or savings required may vary based on exchange rates and individual consulate policy (oh yes, they each have somewhat limited discretion regarding the rules).

The required amounts are calculated per person but some consulates will accept lower financials for a spouse.

We have listed the legal required amounts, as posted by Mexican Immigration. But remember, consulates are not a part of the immigration portfolio. There will be variables at consulates and they are not totally consistent—Bienvenidos a Mexico. Most consulates want original documents.

We recommend you review your Mexican consulate's website and the parameters that they use. Prior to going to a Mexican consulate, please print the online application form and complete it.

The financial requirements for residency are based on multiples of the minimum wage in Mexico. The current government has said they intend to increase the minimum wage 12% a year through their term (until 2030).

The following amounts are based on an exchange rate of 20 to 1 for the US$ and 14 to 1 for the CA$. Consulates vary, even within the US—some consulates are stricter, some are more lenient, and we've seen rates vary a great deal. Please check with your specific consulate to see which rates and amounts they are using. Canadian consulates generally use higher rates than the ones we have quoted. However, as Canadians, you are allowed to apply at some US consulates. Go figure, but could be to your advantage.

For all supporting financial statements, if the account is in both spouses' names, ensure that both names appear on your statements.

Financial requirements for temporary resident visa

There are three ways to obtain this visa. You need **only one** of these financial benchmarks to qualify:

- **Investments or savings:** 12 months of statements showing minimum balances of US$69,750/CA$99,643 (5,000 days x minimum wage MX$279).
- **Monthly income:** Any employment or pension source showing six months of bank statements with deposits of at least US$4,185/CA$5,979 (300 days x minimum wage MX$279).
- **Home ownership in Mexico:** With a value of MX$11,160,000 (40,000 days x minimum wage MX$279) per person. You'll need the original and a copy of the deed. If two people are on the title, the home value needs to be double.

Permanent resident visa

You need **only one** of these financial benchmarks to qualify:

- **Investments or savings:** You must show 12 months of statements with a balance of approximately US$279,000/CA$398,571 (20,000 days x minimum wage MX$279).
- **Monthly income:** Pension-sourced only and you must show six months of bank statements with monthly deposits of US$6,975/CA$9,964 (500 days x minimum wage MX$279).

Additional consulate requirements

- One recent passport-size photograph measuring 39 x 31 mm, face uncovered, no eyeglasses, frontal view, in color and with white background.

- In USA, US$55 cash per person (in Canada, CA$81—EU varies).

- Mexican consulate visa application form to be printed, double-sided, one per person. Complete and take with you. On question 21, for a temporary resident pre-approval, check 'more than 180 days and less than 4 years' and for permanent resident, check 'definitive'. Complete questions 1–25 and nothing more. Please do not sign.

- Your passport

- Financials—12 months of individual printouts for savings/ investments and/or 6 months of individual bank printouts showing income and/or proof of home ownership in Mexico. Take as much proof of financials as possible. You cannot have too much.

- Appointment confirmation form.

Visa application

When you enter the country, you will receive a stamp in your passport that will indicate your arrival date and be marked CANJE. Within 30 days, you must present yourself to Immigration for processing. Where it used to take at least 3–4 weeks, most locations will process your card within two weeks.

The process includes signature, bank payment, photos, fingerprinting and eye scans. Your visa will be issued for one year on the first round. Up to one month before expiration you may renew for one, two or three more years. Your expiration date will be on the anniversary of the day you entered Mexico and received your visa. After four years you may become a permanent resident by merely filling out the paperwork and paying your fees.

When you arrive at your destination—run, don't walk, to the nearest INM (Instituto Nacional de Migración) office. It's a process much easier done with the assistance of a facilitator—in San Miguel, Puerto Vallarta and Mexico City see www.SoniaDiazMexico.com—but if you understand Spanish fairly well, you can muddle through yourself. Maybe. But facilitators are not expensive and I highly recommend that you take advantage of their knowledge, experience and relationships with the local immigration staff. It will make your life a lot easier.

Current visa fees (in pesos)

Always confirm these fees—things can change quickly in Mexico.

Temporary resident:
- **1 year:** MX$5,570
- **2 years:** MX$8,347
- **3 years:** MX$10,571
- **4 years:** MX$12,529

Permanent resident:
- MX$6,789 plus a review fee of MX$1,780 if you are becoming permanent after 4 years as a temporary resident

Work permit (*permiso para trabajar*):
- MX$4,182 (SAT taxation fee not included)

Lost/stolen/damaged visas:
- MX$1,715

Permission to leave while document in process (travel letter):
- MX$569

Ayudita: Never carry a color copy of your visa, driver's license or any other Mexican government-issued ID. That is considered fraud with serious consequences. In Mexico, when not far from home, there is no need to carry your visa. I suggest you save a photo in your phone. You will only need your original when traveling (ditto your passports).

Your spouse and their visa

One visa that *is* possible to apply for from within Mexico is temporary residency for a spouse. But this is where it can get quite complicated. Don't attempt this one on your own.

After one of the spouses obtains a residency visa and resides in Mexico, their significant other can enter the country on a 180-day tourist visa and be processed as a temporary resident under the sponsorship of the resident spouse. The additional amount of income to qualify under this family visa is about MX$8,000 (US$400) a month—but check with your INM office. The additional amount of funds to sponsor a spouse varies from consulate to consulate. At times it may be a little as 25% of the financial requirements for an individual.

It is also possible to sponsor your spouse from inside Mexico once one member of the family becomes a resident—Mexico is extremely family oriented—it is considered a special situation. Now, this is where it gets kind of sticky. If your country is a member of the Apostille Treaty (the USA and Canada are both members), you must have an apostille (in French, apostille means to certify) attached to your marriage certificate to legalize it. US and Canadian notaries can do this.

If your country is not part of the treaty, there will be some other hoops to jump through—please check with your local Mexican consulate for details of how to comply with a non-Apostille country.

And that's just the first sticky part. In Mexico, most people have two last names (their maternal surname and paternal surname). And Mexican women do not take their husbands' surnames.

If you have taken your husband's last name, it's best for you to be the primary applicant and have him come in on the spousal program. Because his last name on the marriage certificate matches his last name on his passport. Yours won't. (Neither will your passport match your birth certificate in this case, which can create other problems.)

The application would be approved because the last names match. But if you do it the other way around and show up with a marriage certificate that shows your maiden name, because you took your husband's name, it is a quagmire to get this sorted out. I know it sounds illogical, but this is my story.

I applied at a small INM office, without a facilitator but with all the prerequisite paperwork, some time before my tourist visa expired. They do take your original passport while processing. In the end, they held it up forever and, one week before I had to leave the country, I had to request to withdraw my application in order to have my passport returned, so that I could leave the country before the last day on my visa. That in itself was a process.

And then I still had to get out of the country, so I went to Guatemala for a few days, and returned and resubmitted. This time, they flat out said no, because my maiden name—the surname shown on our 25+ year-old marriage certificate—was not the same as the surname on my passport, as I had taken my husband's last name 25 years ago. Every piece of ID I owned said 'Wood' was my last name. For 25 years.

They insisted that the two Beverleys were two different people. Despite the fact that the passport, marriage certificate and birth certificate showed identical birthdates and cities of birth and first and middle names. Nope, no go.

What could I do?

They said that if I could get the Canadian Embassy in Mexico City to sign a statement proclaiming that the two Beverleys were one and the same, they would accept that.

And, indeed, the embassy had run up against this before. They asked me to write, in English and Spanish, a declaration that I was one and the same person. I dutifully did this (in English and Spanish, with the help of a translator) using numbers from the passport and the marriage certificate, and assuring all the dots and crosses happened.

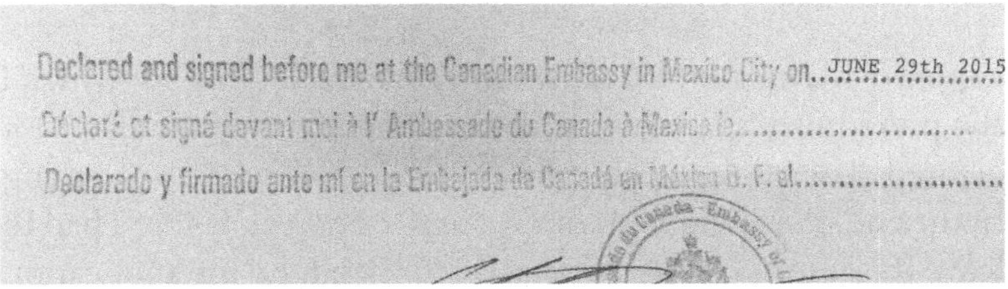
Declared and signed before me at the Canadian Embassy in Mexico City on..JUNE 29th 2015

Déclaré et signé devant moi à l' Ambassade du Canada à Mexico le..........................

Declarado y firmado ante mí en la Embajada de Canadá en México D. F. el.........................

The embassy would then witness me signing the same, authorize it or somehow notarize it, and I would be on my way. A little more complicated than that but it worked, finally. Just not easily. And it helped that by then we had moved to Mexico City, where the INM building is huge and they've seen everything.

My original application was submitted in San Miguel—where we lived at the time—and things are never easy in smaller towns and smaller offices. In the cities, they've seen and dealt with it all before, so there's precedence. Plus, San Miguel's INM office is incredibly busy all the time. In retrospect, I'd have given the whole file over to Sonia from the beginning if I was doing this over.

Do consider having the husband be the one who applies from inside Mexico if you are going this route and you've changed your last name. His name will always be the same.

But it's not even just the last name that can get you in trouble. For example, suppose you didn't take your husband's name. But your passport says 'Mary Elizabeth Smith' and your marriage certificate says 'Mary E Smith'. Your application will be rejected.

If applying from within the country on a family-sponsored visa, it is helpful to have the services of a facilitator, as it can be quite complicated.

Ayudita: If the wife qualifies and the husband enters on a tourist visa as the family member looking to obtain residency from inside the country, this can often be easier. The husband's name on his passport more often matches the name on the marriage license.

Other family visas

Visa through marriage to a Mexican National

This method means no pre-approval at a Mexican consulate outside the country and no financials are required. Probably the easiest visa of all. The process can be started in Mexico. The expat spouse must have a valid tourist visa. It's simpler if the marriage takes place in Mexico, otherwise the marriage license must have an apostille attached or be legalized, and both the license and the apostille must be translated by a certified translator in Mexico. Make it easy on yourself and get married in Mexico!

Visa through children

There is a family visa which allows foreigners with a child born in Mexico to become permanent residents (not temporary residents) by applying in Mexico, with no need to prove financials. Parents need a current tourist visa, the child's Mexican birth certificate and government-issued ID. The names in the parents' passports must be exactly the same name as parents' names on the child's birth certificate.

In addition, the child born in Mexico may sponsor siblings as permanent residents. Or, a parent who has gained residency sponsored by the baby born in Mexico may sponsor other children not born in Mexico. Those other children must be under age 18 and they will be permanent residents.

Expired visas

Perhaps one advantage to a permanent residency is that it never expires—unless you land on the wrong side of the law, in which case you can expect to have whichever visa ripped from your hot little hands. Temporary resident visa expiry dates are written day/month/year. And thus, 11/02/2020 is 11 February 2020—not November 2, 2020. If you waited until November to renew, you would be out of luck.

If your temporary resident card has expired while in Mexico you have 60 days to apply at Immigration. There is a fine. If you are out of country, you may enter Mexico within 55 days of expiration. You must submit your renewal at immigration within five days of returning to Mexico and there is no fine.

Be sure Immigration staff at your point of entry do not record you as a tourist or keep your temporary resident card. In each situation, you are required to prove your financial amounts using the current year's requirements.

If your temporary resident visa has expired by less than 60 days and you are in Mexico you may apply for a temporary resident visa, but you are bounced back to year one. If this is the case, contact a facilitator for assistance, unless your Spanish is fluent and you are well-versed with current immigration laws—and there is a fine.

There are occasional amnesty programs for expired visas (including tourist) but the best defense, however, is a good offence. Understand what the dates are on your visa and you won't face this major inconvenience.

Ayudita: The visa expiration date is written day/month/year. In the US, dates are written month/day/year. Pay close attention. You do *not* want your visa to expire because you read the expiry date wrong.

Lost resident card

If you lose your temporary or permanent resident card while outside of Mexico you may go to the nearest Mexican consulate. Another option is to immediately go to Immigration at the airport upon arrival in Mexico—request a meeting and a two-page letter called *Acta De Internacion Aerea*.

You then apply at your local INM in Mexico. If immigration at the airport records you as a tourist, that is what you will be and you will have to start your visa process over again at a Mexican consulate and prove your financial status again.

The working life—will you continue to work?

Working outside Mexico

If you are only semi-retired (or not retired at all) and work for companies outside Mexico, you do not have to report this income to Mexico and you do not have to have a special visa with work permission. As long as you work remotely—online, by phone, however—and your money is paid to you outside the country, no problem. One may not earn Mexican-sourced income as a temporary resident but you may earn income from outside of Mexico.

Working inside Mexico and earning income in local currency

A tourist may not earn income sourced in Mexico.

To earn income, you must have an RFC (Registro Federal de Contribuyentes) number. In fact, all residents of Mexico are required to have one. The federal government mandates that every resident aged 18 and older must register with the SAT and obtain an RFC, regardless of their income or tax status. Your RFC serves as a personal tax identification number issued by the SAT.

This is an attempt to control corruption and money laundering. The RFC is typically needed for various transactions, such as opening a bank account, purchasing a vehicle, signing up for utilities, or buying/selling property. It is also required to qualify for a capital gains exemption when selling property and is mandatory for renting out property or performing any kind of work in Mexico, including artistic or musical work. Tourists cannot obtain an RFC—only residents are eligible.

Temporary residents who wish to earn income in Mexico must apply for a work visa, officially known as a *permiso para trabajar*. Examples of types of income include being a landlord, selling art, paid performing (musician, acting, singer), realtor, opening a business, providing paid services (massage, hair stylist, consulting), among other vocations. To obtain a work visa, you must first register with the SAT for tax purposes. An accountant should do this to ensure the correct income category is selected.

Once you have registered for the *permiso para trabajar*, you must immediately apply for a new temporary resident status. There is no grace period—you cannot earn income sourced in Mexico until the new status has been processed.

A permanent resident may work but, again, you must register with SAT and inform Immigration—however, when you are permanent, you have 90 days to do so, and you may earn income during this time. On a few rare occasions, you may still be denied permission.

Failure to register with Immigration within the times will lead to a fine and, in some instances, deportation. When you are renewing residency at Immigration, staff check with SAT's database (taxation office akin to IRS and Revenue Canada). They can determine if you have an RFC number and if your RFC is registered for a business (including being a landlord).

If you wish to work for a Mexican company as an employee, this is yet another process—the company should provide assistance in obtaining the valid permissions.

And, don't forget, the tax rules in your home country still apply in many cases.

Chapter 10:

Bringing your stuff and your pets

Moving household goods

Moving your furniture, art and assorted household goods to Mexico involves special requirements and documentation. The goods themselves are restricted to used (not new) items that are normally part of a household, such as furniture, clothing, linens, and appliances.

Minimize problems and fees by learning about all applicable requirements and preparing your documents and shipments accordingly.

To move household goods into Mexico, you must have an immigration status of permanent resident (residente permanente) or temporary resident (residente temporal). To be excluded from the Mexican IVA tax, your items must enter Mexico no later than 6 months from time your visa is fully issued in Mexico.

Temporary resident status is for those moving to Mexico for a limited time, or at least with the intention of moving out of Mexico in the future. If temporary residents move out of Mexico, they must take their household goods with them.

They are also discouraged from selling or giving away their goods while residing in Mexico. By contrast, permanent residents may move out of Mexico and leave their household goods behind.

Here are some of the documents you must provide to bring household goods into Mexico:

- **Resident card:** Official document of temporary or permanent resident status
- **Bill of lading (B/L or BoL):** Required for transporting goods by sea—if shipping by air, this document is known as the air waybill (AWB)
- **Packing list:** Detailed catalog of your goods, including a description and shipping box number for each item
- **Proof of last entry date:** May be an airline ticket or reservation
- **Proof of address:** May be a utility bill dated within three months of your last entry
- **Passport:** From your county of citizenship
- **Letter of declaration to customs:** Including your Mexico address, a description of your goods, and acknowledgment of the requirement to bring your goods with you when you move out of Mexico

- **Letter of empowerment:** Authorizes a customs broker you are working with to handle and transport your goods

- **Declaration of household goods (*declaración para menaje de casa*):** Required only for permanent residents and Mexican citizens—optional but also recommended for temporary residents

Special note for Canadians: It can be expensive to move your household goods because they either need to go by sea or in bond through the USA. Check around on the forums and Facebook pages of groups in the area you are moving to for mom and pop movers. They will have the best prices, but be sure to get personal recommendations.

- **Allowed:** Article 90 of the Mexican customs law states that the items you take across must be used personal items and furniture of a house—for example clothes, books, furniture, appliances and electronics. Tools and implements are also allowed if they are required for your profession or if they are used for a hobby. Medical equipment, such as a wheelchair, blood pressure or sugar monitors and oxygen generators are allowed duty-free. New and unused items and those in unopened packaging may be allowed into Mexico but will likely be subject to duty and other requirements.

- **Not allowed:** Guns or ammunition of any caliber, as well as most other weapons. Also, no fresh or frozen food, plants, spices, or seeds are allowed. While personal medication, supplements, and perfumes or other cosmetics are allowed when carried with your luggage, it is not recommended to ship these items with your household goods. Vehicles, including cars, boats, recreational vehicles and trailers, are not considered household goods and must be declared and approved separately.

Menaje de casa is a permit for the moving of household and personal items to Mexico. It is available from Mexican consulates and is granted to expats who already have a temporary or permanent resident card.

At the consulate, you need a valid photo and temporary or permanent resident card, you must provide your address both outside and inside of Mexico, and provide four copies listing the household items in your shipment.

Your list must contain a detailed description and the quantity of the goods. For electronic items, you must indicate brand, model and serial number. The fee for the *menaje de casa* permit ranges from US$127–185. The tax exemption is only valid for the first 6 months after you receive your residency card.

Ayudita: Birth certificates are often required in Mexico. When coming to reside in Mexico, please bring your birth certificate.

Bringing pets with you

You are allowed to bring two pets (dogs or cats) per person. Beyond this limit, a fee applies. While a health certificate is no longer required to enter Mexico with pets, it is recommended to obtain one. Otherwise, the animal will be inspected by SENASICA upon arrival.

Entry by car is generally more relaxed than entry by plane, but it is advisable to have the proper paperwork—just in case.

1. The heath certificate issued by the veterinarian must be on letterhead paper, including the veterinarian's professional license number (or its equivalent), and must indicate that the animal is in good health.

2. You also need proof of vaccines against rabies and distemper, administered at least 15 days before the arrival of your pet in Mexico. Mexico will accept the 3-year vaccine from dogs and cats entering the country from the United States or Canada.

These documents (the originals and one photocopy) should be on letterhead from the vet's office and include:

- Your name and address in your normal country of residence and your planned address in Mexico

- A description of the pet

- The date the pet was vaccinated against rabies and distemper and the vaccination's expiry date.

But that's not all.

3. We also recommend a declaration from the vet that the pet appeared clinically healthy and that the pet has been dewormed internally and externally within 6 months prior to arrival in Mexico.

The process is more formal when arriving by air. If you do not have the required paperwork, you will be given the opportunity to contact a vet in Mexico (at your expense) to come to the port of entry and issue the necessary documents. The most recent account I heard of involved a vet fee of a reasonable MX$800 (US$40).

If all of this is too much for you, there are pet transport companies who can walk you through the process and arrange to send your pets as cargo on your behalf. Not cheap, but what's peace of mind worth? It all depends on what you are comfortable doing yourself.

If you plan to drive your pet(s), the good news is that the process is usually a little more relaxed at the land borders, but you'd better have all your paperwork in order just in case. It would be a shame to have to turn around because you don't have the papers they ask for.

For information on bringing your car into the country, please see *Chapter 11: Transportation*. Yes, that's right, it's so complicated that it gets its own chapter.

Please have a collar and tag on your dog. The tag should include your pet's name and a phone number. If the phone number is not a Mexican number, please include the access code for when calling from Mexico.

Chapter 11:

Transportation

Bringing your vehicle to Mexico on a temporary resident visa

Temporary import permits (TIPs) are controlled by Aduana Mexico (customs) and are needed if you travel outside of the Baja Peninsula or outside the border zones (further than 16 mi from the border). Effective January 1, 2020 vehicle permits are digital and windshield stickers are not issued. Applicants receive a digital copy via email. If you are entering from the south, there is also no need for a TIP in Quintana Roo but you cannot drive from the north through the intervening states without a TIP.

Those entering Mexico with a pre-approved visa from a Mexican consulate must not obtain a TIP online—the process is only for tourists.

For those entering as a pre-approved temporary resident from a Mexican consulate, vehicle permits are issued for the same length as your pre-approval visa—30 days. Within 30 days of entering Mexico you must start your visa process at your local INM office. There is a fee, and a refundable deposit—refundable only if you meet all the requirements below for the time the car is in the country. Please check online for current amounts.

Your next step as a pre-approved temporary resident is to extend your car permit (TIP). This is all very simple to do with the assistance of a facilitator if it's sounding complicated.

Once a Temporary Residency visa is issued, please go to Aduana to extend your TIP. If you do not start your residency visa process within 30 days, it will mean you must start over at a consulate and you and your vehicle are both in Mexico illegally.

You do the same each time you renew your Temporary Resident visa—go to Aduana to extend your TIP. We can help with extending your car permit and protecting your deposit.

You may only request a permit for a vehicle that is registered in your name or that of your spouse, your child or your parent. You must show either a valid title or registration to obtain your TIP.

Recreational vehicles such as motor homes will often receive a 10-year TIP and a deposit is not required—but this is only for tourist visas. If you have temporary residency, your RV is treated as above.

A few tips: Don't drive at night. It's just not worth it. Anything can be on the roads—an airport driver told me about a cow in the middle of the toll road near Mexico City one night. On the toll road!

When driving between cities, always take the toll road if it's an option. It's a perfectly good road and it's regulated by on- and off-ramps and toll booths.

Plus, you're insured when you are on toll roads, and the *Ángeles Verdes* (Green Angels) regularly patrol—a roadside assistance fleet operated by the Mexican Tourism Ministry. The free roads are not in as good condition and it will take you a lot longer to get to where you're going.

Who may drive your foreign-plated car in Mexico?

Vehicles with TIPs can be driven in Mexico by the importer, their spouse, their parents, grandparents, brothers or sisters, children, grandchildren, even if those relatives are Mexican nationals. It may also be driven by any foreigner who is a tourist or temporary resident. These drivers are all permitted without the permit-holder in the vehicle.

However, a Mexican national, such as a maid, gardener, mechanic or bellhop, who is **not** related to you, cannot drive your vehicle without you in the car. And it's serious. There have been cases where cars have been confiscated plus fines issued.

And just as serious—once you are issued your permanent resident visa, you may no longer have a foreign-plated car in the country in your name. The TIP is no longer valid, as your temporary resident visa is gone. You need to plan for this if you have a car in the country on a TIP. 'T' is for temporary.

Ayudita: When travelling, call 078 to reach the Green Angels who patrol Mexican toll roads. They provide mechanical assistance, emergency radio communication, aid in case of accident, advice and route information including maps, and information about services and tourist attractions in the region.

You cannot sell a foreign-plated car in Mexico. For a temporary resident it is recommended you turn in your car permit when you drive out of Mexico, prior to becoming a permanent resident. If you are unable to return the same vehicle across the border (due to total loss, for example), you will have a difficult time having the vehicle removed from the Mexican database. They would consider the vehicle as still being in Mexico and you would forfeit your guarantee deposit and be prohibited from bringing in another vehicle.

That said, you can turn your vehicle in (if it is old, for example, as ours is) to a government authorized depot where they will crush it for scrap. You must pay for this service but at least it's a fair bet that you'll be out of the database—and may even have your deposit returned, but don't hold your breath.

There is also the option of a *retorno seguro* (secured return) for cars that are no longer legal to be driven out of Mexico. It's like a temporary paper license plate and gives you five days to get out of the country. This temporary 'get out of jail free' card is available at your local SAT (tax) office.

Insurance and accidents

Vehicle insurance is required when driving in Mexico. Your policy in Canada or the US will not cover you in Mexico. There are plenty of options if you Google 'Mexican car insurance' and you can purchase online before you depart. It's a lot cheaper—ours is about US$400 a year (for an older car).

But do note: Make sure you get the type of insurance where an adjuster comes out to the scene of the accident, or another representative from the insurance company. Otherwise, you may go to jail until they determine whose fault the accident is, whether anyone is hurt or not. The insurance company attends the scene of the accident and guarantees payment if you are found to be at fault and that is enough to release you.

If you are in a car accident, the cars are not moved until the insurance adjuster comes. It's very important that in any car accident, you stay at the scene of the accident until the adjuster and/or the authorities arrive. If both cars have insurance and the adjusters of each company agree who is responsible, then the cars can be moved to a place where they do not block traffic.

And as of June 1, 2016, if anyone is injured in an accident and requires medical treatment, all the drivers involved go to jail until fault is determined. That is normally 48–72 hours.

Mexican laws states that if there is any person injured, both drivers will be held in the *Ministerio Público* offices (like a small jail) until the authorities can declare who is responsible for the accident. If you are involved in a car accident where someone is injured, call the insurance company immediately—they will provide legal assistance. You'll still be held, however, until culpability is determined.

Purchasing a used vehicle with Mexican plates

This is always a risky proposition. But the most important thing to note is that the original *factura* (bill of sale)—the one from when the vehicle was brand new—follows the vehicle for the life of the vehicle.

Every seller must sign the back of the factura. Without the original factura, even if the car is 20 years old, you cannot register the vehicle. There's lots of shady stuff going on but if you buy from a dealership and the paperwork is in order, you should be fine. Just be really careful and do your due diligence before purchasing.

To register a car you buy in Mexico, most states will want you to have a Mexican driver's license.

Getting your Mexican driver's license

Getting your Mexican driver's license is a relatively easy procedure. It varies from state to state but primarily consists of an eye exam and, occasionally, a multiple choice 10-question exam on a computer. In some states, when you present your gringo driver's license, they will just give you one. But there are also places that will require you to take a short physical test as well as a written test. Do some Googling on your state or town. They do require your blood type so know it or be prepared to go for a blood test. And bring your own pen. Also:

- Original and copy of your passport photo page
- Original and copy of your immigration document/visa card
- Original and copy of electric, water or phone bill from your casa

You should study up a bit first—making a right on a red light is illegal unless there is an arrow indicating that you may do so. There are other regional practices, such as in rural areas (not cities), pulling over to the right shoulder and waiting for traffic to pass before making a left-hand turn. And of course, all road signs are in Spanish so you will need to understand what they mean, whether you are on a Mexican license or a gringo one.

There are topes. These are speed bumps and they are everywhere. Sometimes they are marked, sometimes they aren't. Watch for them.

It's preferable to have a Mexican license for driving in Mexico—keep your non-Mexican license for driving when north and your Mexican license when driving in Mexico. The last thing you want is for a police officer to keep your Canadian or American license as a way to demand some cash (which happens occasionally).

We should also note that while technically you are legally required to stop at a stop sign—it's rarely done. They're considered more as an advisory. If no one is there, you don't have to stop. And if you do and there's a car behind you, well... you have interrupted 'the flow'. You'll understand what we mean after you've lived here a while. Just be extra defensive when you drive and do not expect people to stop for stop signs. Silly rabbit.

Ubers, taxis, buses and planes

Big topic. Many Mexican cities and towns have Uber—from Guadalajara to Cuernavaca (and more). It's an inexpensive way to get around, and it's secure. You're given the car, the make, the license plate, the driver's confirmed name and photo—and there's a GPS marker of where you are at all times.

You pay automatically online, although it's nice to give them a cash tip in pesos. Remember, Uber takes 30% of the fee you pay, so these guys and gals don't make a lot of money. Tips are much appreciated.

The same for taxi drivers—the rates are reasonable although it's always wise to ask how much before you get in. But the tips are important and appreciated. Always call and have your taxi dispatched to you or take a cab from the *sitios* (cab stands) which are ubiquitous in every town. Never flag one. You have no idea who is driving.

There are private drivers with new cars who also aren't expensive and are much more reliable than taxis (many are Uber drivers who drive privately on the side). The local gringo message lists and forums can offer suggestions on where to find reliable drivers.

For longer trips, even Uber will cost too much, so you'll have to turn to buses and planes. There are many executive bus lines (each line covers a different route/region) and they are awesome buses. They have internet, first-run movies (in Spanish but occasionally in English with subtitles)—and you get either a snack or a meal (sandwich) depending on the duration and a beverage (juice, water, soda). There are men's and women's washrooms aboard in the back. It's almost like flying.

Speaking of flying—that's also a great way to get around inside Mexico. If you watch for sales, Volaris has some incredible pricing. We have always found Aeroméxico to be expensive, but others like them. As a rule, domestic flights can be quite affordable if you watch for sales.

And always check Volaris and Aeroméxico for international flights. They don't show up on most of the aggregators so go directly to their website. Volaris is always putting on 50% sales and has direct flights to many US and Canadian cities. If you're in Canada, don't forget WestJet either—they fly directly from Canada to many Mexican destinations.

But, in closing, back to cars and driving. Because we have dogs, we worry about not having a vehicle in case of an emergency if we need to get to the vet in a hurry. Other than that, I wouldn't even bother with a vehicle in Mexico unless you are living in a rural area. It can be complicated. And it could get expensive if you are ever in a serious accident.

Chapter 12:

Communications

Communications in Mexico are generally inexpensive and highly functional. It's easy to get a cell phone and it's cheap—MX$300 (US$15) a month gives you nationwide coverage in Mexico with unlimited data and calls to North American numbers. And you'll be in and out of the shop in minutes.

Ayudita: You can even call US and Canadian toll-free numbers from local Mexican telephones—it simply requires substituting a few numbers. See our toll-free telephone substitution chart in *Chapter 24: Handy guides*.

You can get a home provider package with a home phone (unlimited North American and some European and Asian calls), internet and cable TV for MX$1,000 (US$50). Sure, you might want to add channels to that, but it doesn't get very expensive.

Staying in touch with people at home is simple—between free calls on landlines and cell phones, there's Skype, Zoom, WhatsApp, Facebook—and all have phone functions. Not to mention FaceTime. Vonage is still popular (a 'voice over internet protocol' or VoIP line) and people can dial a local number to reach you. Technology is so advanced and forwarding calls, emails, voicemails and more is so easy, you should have no trouble staying in touch.

That said, if you move into a gringo area that doesn't have the infrastructure to support the growth, or a tourist area that doubles in population during holidays and weekends, you'll get internet slowdowns. And the more rural you are, the less service you'll get—both cell service and internet. There are trade-offs, but good internet can really make your life a lot more pleasant.

We've been lucky—internet is important to us and for the last several years, we've chosen locations with fiber-optic connections available. We've also set up accounts with two providers—that way, if one is down, chances are the other is up and running. If your job depends on it, you should too.

I'll go even further—get on the Mexican gringo forums and email lists and ask about the availability of reliable, fast internet. I have heard some mutterings on the Lake Chapala/Ajijic Facebook groups about waiting for weeks to have service installed. And the influx of snowbirds in the winter severely strains the system. It is primarily those who are using the telephone system (Telmex) for their service who have the most trouble, but sometimes it's the only choice.

I'm sure installation problems come and go, but you don't want to be landing in town while they're happening and waiting a month to get online. Or spending all day, every day, online at Starbucks. That's a lot of lattes. There are cable companies that supply telephone, internet and television. Most of the trouble with infrastructure issues seems to be Telmex (which makes sense, as their lines are the oldest).

US and Canadian satellite services are available if you want to have the same TV you had at home. Otherwise, the local cable is primarily in Spanish, but you can set up subtitles and there are English language shows with Spanish subtitles on occasion—perhaps 5–6% of the lineup.

But what do you need from cable these days other than internet? You've got all the other television options like Netflix, Amazon Prime and much more. You can even subscribe directly to US networks ABC, CBS and NBC online and watch their shows ad-free.

That said, these are all delivered via internet connection so we're back to the issue of making sure you get good internet. Do your research. Look for an area to live that has fiber-optic internet delivery. And buy a big gulp plan. You won't be sorry.

Snail mail services

Towns with significant gringo populations will have mail forwarding offices. They will supply a unique US address, usually in a Texas border town, which you can use as your address of record. Your mail will be picked up and delivered to a central office in your town in Mexico at least several times a week and possibly daily. Check the local internet groups and Facebook pages for locations.

If you aren't in a gringo town, there are still services for you—America Ship (www.america-ship.com) is one. You get a free address in Texas but there's no regular delivery. You can stockpile your packages and mail until you feel you have a worthwhile pile and they'll send it to you via courier. Overall the price isn't bad but, clearly, it's not as convenient as it is in towns with larger expat populations. You give up some things to get other things—just depends on what's important to you.

The other alternative is to use a family member or friend's address for a mail drop. Or a mail drop in your home town. We have a mail drop in Canada that scans our incoming mail and sends it to us via email. We then determine if it's worth forwarding. We're back so often that we just ask them to hold it until our return, unless it's something urgent like a replacement credit card.

You'll find something that works for you—there are many options.

Chapter 13:

Should I rent or buy?

While it's prudent to rent before you buy, we bought our first house only three months after landing in San Miguel de Allende. Now, that said, we also knew that there is (almost) always a large demand by gringos for houses in that town so if we changed our minds, the market was pretty liquid. Have a look around online before you do either—and familiarize yourself with neighborhoods and prices.

The joys of renting

If you are not in a high-turnover gringo area, I strongly recommend that you do rent for at least a year and experience all the seasons—and get to know the neighborhoods—before purchasing.

In non-gringo enclaves and neighborhoods, it can often take a year to sell a home (or more).

In our case in San Miguel, it took three months. Other towns for quick sales (in the correct neighborhoods) are Puerto Vallarta, Ajijic, Cabo, Cancún. Almost anywhere with big gringo communities has rapid real estate turnover (many come, stay a few years, and then go home). The real estate market everywhere, except the smallest towns, is fairly steady but the fast sales are in gringo towns. Our house in Cuernavaca, with a very limited gringo population, took two years to sell.

But, back to the renting concept. To begin with, take a short-term (one or two month) rental that you find online—anywhere from Craigslist to AirBnB to HomeAway to VRBO—there are a multitude of places to look. And once you are in situ, assess the communities and the neighborhoods available to you before renting long-term.

It's all location, location, location—are there the right number of tiendas (corner stores), what is the building orientation with regard to the sun, where is the closest church? That last one has nothing to do with being religious. If you're close to a church, there will be fiesta after fiesta and lots of noise in the tourist towns. Are there parks in the neighborhood, do you feel safe, are you walking distance to anywhere or will you have to drive? All things to consider before signing any kind of a longer-term lease.

If you are in a gringo town, there will be an internet group you can join. This is one place to find longer term rentals. Also, the local newspaper, which may or may not be available in English. Word of mouth, signs on doors—*se renta*—keep your eyes and ears open. Every town has a property management company that handles rentals.

You can use Google Translate to participate in Spanish language rental groups online—just admit that you're using Google Translate and excuse yourself, and you'll be welcomed.

Rental costs will vary based on the size of the house, the location, furnished or unfurnished, utilities included or extra—there are many variables. If it's a gringo rental, it will almost always be more expensive than a Mexican rental.

If you're renting from another gringo, chances are that they will price in US dollars. While they can do that, they have to be willing to accept the equivalent in pesos for the actual exchange—or you can pay them USD if you have it and want to.

I know people who have rented perfectly charming one-bedroom *casitas* in lush garden settings for the equivalent of US$300. And I know people who have rented seven-bedroom houses in the high-end of town with five staff for US$10,000 a month. These are the extremes—but they range from one to the other. Out of town, of course, is always cheaper than in town. Do some research, but as a rule—anywhere from US$1,000 a month and up will get you a reasonable two- or three-bedroom home.

Houses are different than they are north of the border. The utilities operate differently, the service people operate differently.

Gas

Each home has its own propane tank. There are no natural gas lines like up north. A gas tanker comes to your house occasionally to fill it. Cooking is done with gas, as is hot water heating—and you can purchase gas clothes dryers. You'll want to use as little electric power as possible, as it's billed on a sliding scale, so gas appliances are a good idea.

Power

CFE (Comisión Federal de Electricidad) is a federal institution that is in charge of production and distribution of power in the country. Like death and taxes, you can't avoid them. Power bills are based on a subsidized tier system. You are penalized for higher usage. If you decide to live on the beach and want air conditioning and you are paying for the utilities, it can get pricey. That said, air conditioning is not required in many places in Mexico. In addition, be prepared for power surges and loss of power all over Mexico during the rainy season when there are major storms. Buying surge protectors and voltage regulators for your electronics is advised—or just buy an uninterruptible power supply (UPS) which takes care of both.

Water

Many Mexican homes have a *tinaco* (water tank) on the roof to hold water and the water system is fed by gravity. In addition, they will often have an underground cistern to hold water, which is pumped up to the tinaco as required. While the city supplies water, it is not direct to residential faucets the way it is north of the border. It comes to your cistern at times during the week and you store it until you need it. And because it's not a pressurized system (although some newer gringo houses do add pressurized water), no paper products go in the toilet. That's the ubiquitous mini wastebasket in most Mexican bathrooms.

Also, you do not drink this water. Many homes have an intake filter or under-sink filter to provide potable drinking water. Otherwise, you have regular delivery of *garrafones* of purified water.

Heating and air conditioning

There are very few homes in Mexico with central heating or air conditioning. You will find units in individual rooms. For heat, people use fireplaces (wood-burning or gas) or portable heaters with relatively low power draws. Air conditioning can be expensive but if you are in a place that requires it, you likely have the sunshine to support a solar system. All of Mexico, in theory, could support a solar system and great strides are being made in this direction.

Location, location, location

Check it out before you commit. Are there tiendas (local stores)? While convenient, they can also be places that teens hang out on weekend nights. You might not want to be right next door to one. Harmless, for the most part, but not quiet. And speaking of noise! That gorgeous colonial church across the street that makes your 2nd floor view look like a postcard? They'll be letting off loud *cohetes* (bottle rockets—fireworks with no visuals) at 5am on fiesta days to wake up the sun. And did we mention marching bands? They all end up at the church! You'll also have roosters, barking dogs and occasional loud music until 6am. Bienvenidos a Mexico.

What to check before committing long term:

- Test your cell service and internet service. Signals do not pass well through concrete.

- Check the faucets on all the showers and sinks for water pressure and for hot water. Flush the toilets.

- Come to the neighborhood at different hours to check the noise levels.

- Make sure you know who is paying for the utilities—you or the owner? Internet, cable, water, power, gas and maid/gardener services for starters.

- Are the appliances included? They aren't always.

Leases in Mexico are not legal unless they are written in Spanish. Mexican landlords do not pay for repairs the way gringo landlords do. In fact, your lease will probably say something to the effect that any repairs up to MX$5,000 (US$250) are the responsibility of the tenant. You are always better off, at least for your first rental, to work with an English-speaking real estate agent. They get their commission from the owner, so are free to use and know all the ins and outs of Mexican rentals.

Chapter 14:

Can I get healthcare?

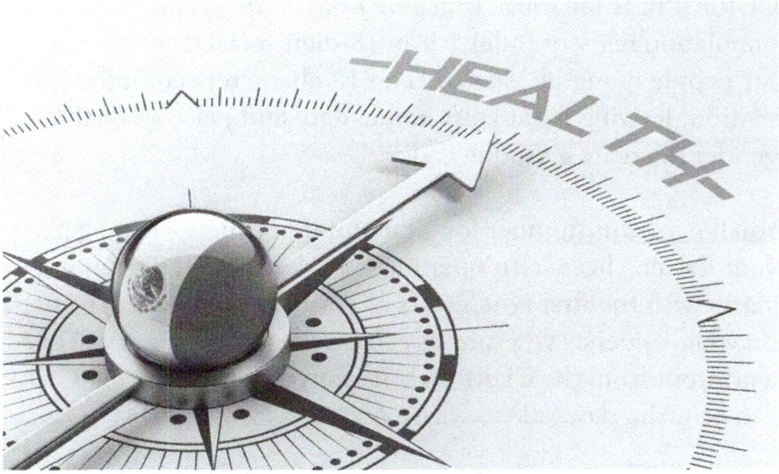

There are basically four healthcare paths available—private insurance, INSABI (formerly Seguro Popular), IMSS (more for workers' benefits, but some expats can qualify) and cash.

I don't recommend cash as a plan for emergency treatment—that works fine for regular doctor visits and small health issues but it can get pricey if you are in need of emergency care. Nothing like US costs, but an emergency appendectomy in a private hospital will run you the equivalent of US$5,000. Overnight in a hospital (imagine a car accident) works out to about US$1,000 a night. You can go broke pretty quickly. And don't count on an air ambulance to take you home to your home country medical care—you may not be well enough to be moved.

INSABI (formerly Seguro Popular)

Seguro Popular was a public health insurance program that was replaced in 2020 with INSABI (Institute of Health for Welfare). Anyone who has a CURP number is eligible. This includes all legal temporary and permanent residents.

CURP stands for *Clave Única de Registro de Población* (unique population registry code). It's an 18-digit social security number for people living in Mexico. The 18 characters combine information deriving from your name, date and place of birth, and gender to create a unique code.

You'll need this number for all manner of things—from getting your driver's license to opening a bank account. This number starts with the first two letters of your surname and is printed on your residency visa card (green card). However, you will need a printout from the CURP website for your INSABI. Your CURP can be printed out at www.gob.mx/curp.

If you know your CURP number, select '*Clave Única de Registro de Población*' and where it says '*Ingresa tu Curp*' enter your CURP number and then select '*Buscar*'. Your CURP will download and you then you can print it out.

If you do not know your CURP number select '*Datos Personales*'. There are times you may have a number and not be aware you do. Insert your first and middle names where it says '*Nombre(s)*' and surname where it says '*Primer apellido*'. Then insert your birth date, month and year. Finally, in the drop-down box in the list of states at the bottom select '*Nacido en el extranjero*'. Then select '*Buscar*'. Your CURP will download and you can print it out.

So now you have your CURP print-out and you are good to go. There is no fee for INSABI. There is no sign-up. One needs a

CURP print-out and photo ID such as passport or temporary or permanent resident visa. There is no membership and no age limit. You simply go to what was a Seguro Popular facility for healthcare with the two documents and present them at the reception.

IMSS

IMSS is also a government healthcare program mostly for employees, but some expats who are temporary or permanent residents join. The annual fee is MX$7,000–9,000 (US$350–450) per person, depending on age, and renewed annually. Those with pre-existing conditions are normally declined. In your first year, the coverage is almost non-existent but the second year is much better and subsequent years provide full coverage. It is primarily used by people legally working in Mexico.

Private insurance

Private health insurance is widely available both from Mexican companies and companies around the world. Some pre-existing conditions can be covered at a (much) higher cost. It's basically worldwide medical coverage for expats, excluding the USA. Even with a US$1,000 deductible, it's affordable until you hit 65, then it will likely double. And it will double again at 70. You'll find many expats going home around this age because the private medical care becomes unaffordable.

Some of the companies you can Google to check are Allianz, AXA, Bupa, GNP Seguros and many others—none are more recommended than another and it's up to you to do your due diligence, check prices and coverage of each. Also, it really helps if you can have your insurance company pay your hospital directly. Check to see if they do this—and if they have 'approved' hospitals, with whom they have contracts, in your area.

We had international insurance, worldwide except USA, sold to us by a company in the US (the reps were in Mexico, expats themselves). We really weren't thinking. When my husband was recently hospitalized for gall bladder trouble, we submitted our claim which we had paid ourselves in Mexican pesos. They adjusted it to US dollars and sent it to our Canadian bank account. So, we paid exchange fees from pesos (what we paid) to US dollars (their reimbursement currency) to Canadian dollars (our bank account). Really stupid.

And outrageous wire fees—instead of processing all small claims together, we were paying a US$15 wire fee on every claim, which they processed separately (such as a US$44 prescription drug claim). And taking three months to pay. And they aren't cheap. I wasn't impressed with them, to be honest, until my husband required a back operation.

Because it was international insurance, good everywhere but the USA, he flew to Canada for a very expensive back operation in a private clinic. It was authorized ahead of time and we didn't have to pull out a credit card.

That was in late 2019, just before COVID, which pushed that company into bankruptcy. Today, we are paying more than US$8,000 a year, almost CA$10,000 for health insurance with $5,000 deductible. I'm sure that sounds perfectly rational if you are American—but we're from Canada (and still Canadian residents for tax purposes, so we pay our dues), where single-payer insurance rules. Our rates pretty much doubled when my husband turned 65. It's scheduled to double again when I do. And will again when he turns 70. So, you can see how this is playing a to a losing hand.

If you are looking for private insurance (if you can afford it, it's good to have), I would suggest one of the Mexican companies.

Private healthcare is incredible in Mexico. But US-based world-wide health insurance? For our purposes, not so great.

Ayudita: No matter how you pay for your medical treatment, your records are yours to maintain. Do not expect doctors or hospitals to have records on your last treatment. You get copies of all imaging and all reports—keep them because you'll need them next time.

Self-insuring (paying cash)

I hear people say they plan to self-insure because the costs of insurance are so high. Believe me, paying $5,000 or even $10,000 a year is not high compared to the possible debt you will incur if you grow ill. You need to factor health insurance into your budget, even if it is just public care.

I just read another horror story. A couple came to Mexico intending to self-insure. Wife had a heart attack and needed a stent (US$15,000). A few weeks later, they found another blood clot (another US$15,000). Having spent US$30,000 in their first six weeks of their new life, they are now heading home.

We, ourselves, had a situation in the first few months. We'd arrived with our two-years of Canadian (British Columbia, in this case) health insurance intact—you must register, but you can be out of the country up to two years every five years, and still maintain your health insurance in BC. Because it will cover out-of-country medical procedures (when required), we didn't think twice about adding extra insurance.

My husband had an emergency appendectomy. I called our health insurance and they said no problem, pay the bill and we will reimburse you. So, we paid our US$5,000 (great care, by the way, in a private hospital in San Miguel) and submitted the bills. And waited. And waited.

We were reimbursed CA$1,800 about six months later—about US$1,400 at the time. Yup, that's all they said it would have cost to take out an appendix in Canada, and that's all they paid. So, don't think your Canadian healthcare will cover you. It's woefully inadequate and we were lucky it wasn't something larger.

We also know a gentleman who was hospitalized quite suddenly in Puerto Vallarta with some form of sepsis and was in hospital three weeks. His total bill was more than US$100,000 and he needed to cash in retirement savings to pay the bill. Don't play that game. Self-insuring is not safe. If you can't afford insurance, you can't afford to get sick in Mexico. If you live in Mexico legally, you will have access to IMSS-Bienestar for catastrophic events. While it provides basic care that can save your life in an emergency, you may wish to consider private insurance if you can afford it. More expats return home because of medical issues than for any other reason. Don't let it take you by surprise.

Emergency preparedness

If you live on your own, regardless of age, you need to have an emergency plan in an obvious place. Include your medications, emergency contact and the exact location of where you live, including house number and street name, cross streets and house color. Post this near your front door—if you or someone else needs to call the police or an ambulance, they need this information. On some streets, the same house number may repeat itself two, three or more times. And leave detailed instructions to arrange care for any pets.

Keep in mind that private hospitals are expensive and if you have no insurance, you need some financial resources available immediately. And, even with insurance, most want a large hold on your charge card and even payment until your insurance provider pays.

As a temporary or permanent resident, you do have free government healthcare (INSABI). While it may not be your first choice, many 'Hospital Generals' (which is what all hospitals under INSABI are called) have some very good doctors.

People all want some independence but, at the same time and especially as you age, you need a backup plan. You need to have some way to pay for your care, including medications, doctors, transportation, possibly home help and physical therapy. And you need friends or family members available on short notice.

We have heard (and seen) horror stories relating to unexpected events such as broken bones, hip replacements, Alzheimer's, cancer etc. Be prepared, especially when you live alone.

Some further advice (from our readers, with thanks):

- *"I carry in my purse my primary doctor's name and number and a list of the prescription medications that I take. And emergency contact info."*

- *"Make arrangements with a neighbor to check in by phone or email every morning. 'I'm fine' is enough. Exchange keys with that neighbor."*

Prescription drugs

Prescription drug names in Mexico are often different than in the US and Canada. That can be a shock when you try to renew a prescription. We have included a chart listing drug names in all three countries in *Chapter 24: Handy guides*.

Many prescription drugs can be purchased at Mexican pharmacies (farmacias) without prescriptions. Many, but not all. A doctor must prescribe antibiotics (they are surprisingly and refreshingly restrictive with antibiotic prescriptions) and all scheduled drugs such as narcotics, tranquilizers and sleeping medications. These are the big no-nos in Mexico without a prescription and they are considered to be very serious drugs.

Many pharmacies are owned by doctors or have doctors on staff. So, if you've got flu-like symptoms and need medication, your one-stop shop is your local farmacia. They can help you choose the right medication.

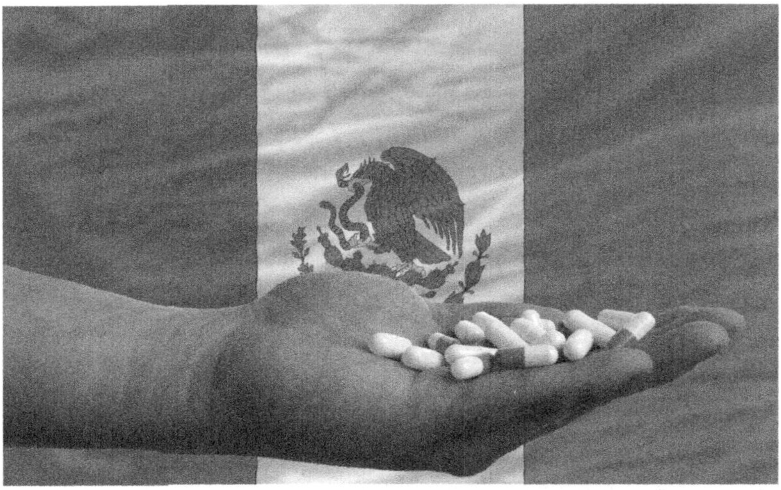

If you wish to bring prescription drugs with you, it is advised you stay away from antibiotics (you shouldn't be traveling anyway), narcotics, tranquilizers and sleeping pills. Any psychotropics such as Valium, or opiate derivatives (such as codeine) will raise red flags and are best left at home. If you really need them, find a Mexican doctor to prescribe them.

Otherwise, you are allowed to bring three months worth of prescription drugs into Mexico, with your prescription. It's unlikely that any of this will be checked at customs, particularly if you are crossing by land—but it's better to be safe than sorry. Have your ducks in a row and all your paperwork at hand.

After your arrival, you are unable to import drugs (or supplements) by mail or courier into Mexico without a special permit from COFEPRIS (the Mexico Ministry of Health).

Marijuana in Mexico

Pot laws have been in limbo in Mexico pretty much since 2009, when personal possession of small amounts was decriminalized. In 2018, the ban on recreational use was ruled unconstitutional, but the clarification of recreational regulations stalled. Medicinal marijuana with less than 1% THC content is legal.

A 2021 Supreme Court ruling legalized recreational use but introduced a significant caveat—permits are still required. However, COFEPRIS, the health regulatory agency, has yet to establish a process for obtaining these permits, leaving recreational users in a legal gray area.

Adults over 18 can legally possess up to 28 grams and grow up to six plants at home, but the absence of a formal regulatory framework creates uncertainty. Possession is technically legal, but purchasing is not, emphasizing the urgent need for clear regulations.

Since the ban on recreational use is unconstitutional, but the law as written has not been changed, it's technically illegal and legal—Schrodinger's pot law. Keep your head down and no one should bother you until it's officially on the books and available on some retail level.

CBD products (cannabidiol, a non-psychoactive compound with medicinal value) are legal in Mexico. As of November 2018, CBD is available in creams, food supplements, foods, and cosmetics without a prescription—provided the THC content is under 1%. Medicinal marijuana with more than 1% THC is also available but requires a prescription from a Mexican doctor.

Do **not** bring any marijuana across the border or you will be jailed. End of story. Once you arrive and are settled in your location of choice, it's okay to make some discreet inquiries—it's clear that it will become legal in the foreseeable future. Just don't be an idiot about it. Things are always changing and certainly the laws, so this section will be updated as new information becomes available.

Chapter 15:

Hiring household employees

Having help with things like housework and gardening at very reasonable rates is one of the perks of living in Mexico. But it's not like some of the stories you hear—about how someone pays the equivalent of US$15 a day for eight hours of cleaning. Those types of employers may exist, as that is the minimum wage in Mexico for nine-hours of work at MX$279 per day, but those employers aren't nice people.

The going rates for household help run from MX$300 (US$15) a day in the poorest areas to MX$600 (US$30) a day. Of course, it depends on the number of days per week and the workload. We, for example, have one person, one day a week and we feel that it's fair to pay MX$500 (US$25) for that one day of services. Others we know pay MX$600 (US$30) a day, but bring them in 6 days a week.

Check the going rate in the area you will settle in. If you want to check out the employee's ability, start them out a lower rate with the intention of giving them a raise if they do a good job and you are comfortable with them. There are all kinds of variables. Some things, however, are the law. But seriously, if you can afford more than minimum wage, please pay your help reasonable wages.

Employee social security

Employees are entitled to social security, the bulk of which is paid by the employer and is based on employee's weekly wage. The employee pays a minor portion, which is retained weekly by employer. Most employers retain an accountant to determine amounts and process.

As of 2023, these benefits now apply to all employees, full or part-time, including maids and gardeners. The calculations are somewhat complex, and the services of a Mexican accountant are advised—at least for the first few years until you get accustomed to Mexican red tape. Their services are quite reasonable and can save you a lot of grief and money.

There are three components to social security—IMSS healthcare, AFORES seniors' pension and INFONAVIT housing.

- **IMSS (*Instituto Mexicano del Seguro Social*):** Government healthcare supported by employers. For employees it provides full health coverage including medical clinics, hospitals, medications and dentists.

- **AFORE (*Administradoras de Fondos para el Retiro*):** Similar to US Social Security or Canada Pension Plan (CPP) and is based on contributions related to an employee's wage and years of employment. Compared to foreign standards it is not a lot of pension income, but certainly important for retired seniors.

- INFONAVIT (***Instituto del Fondo Nacional de la Vivienda para los Trabajadores***): Started in 1972, it provides homes to Mexicans who otherwise could not qualify for financing or save for a down payment. The interest is extremely low. The amount one qualifies for is based on their wage and duration of employment reported by the employer. After time, a person qualifies for assistance.

An employee making, for example, MX$1,000 (US$50) a week would cost the employer approximately MX$800 (US$40) a month for social security coverage. It is important employees are provided social security it must be based on the amount of their full wages. The ramifications for the employer are huge if this is not complied with.

Employee contracts

It is very important to have employee contracts. At some point you may need to be able to prove when an employee commenced employment, the wage rate, the hours of work, the days worked, the duties of the employee and other specifics. There are many things that should be part of a contract for your own protection. If there is ever an employee performance issue, a contract will protect you.

Mexican government labor boards, where employees can file disputes, are usually very pro-employee. Settlements of tens of thousands of pesos are not uncommon.

Sonia prepares employment contracts and termination letters for clients all over Mexico and she can deliver the contract to you online after consultation—see www.SoniaDiazMexico.com to find out more.

Paid vacation

Vacation leave must be paid in cash either before the vacation, or before the end of the year if no vacation has been taken.

To calculate the amount, divide the number of days worked during the past year by 365. Multiply that figure by the number of vacation days due x 1.25 x daily pay to determine the amount of the vacation pay due.

Example: You have an employee working for one year who works one day a week making MX$300: 52 days worked / 365 x 6 days due x 1.25 x 300 daily pay = MX$321 vacation pay.

The number of vacation days due for this calculation is set out by the government as follows:

- **Year 1:** 12 days
- **Year 2:** 14 days
- **Year 3:** 16 days
- **Year 4:** 18 days
- **Year 5:** 20 days
- **Year 10:** 22 days
- **Year 15:** 24 days

For every year the employee continues to work for the employer, he/she will receive an additional two days off. After the fifth year, the employee's vacation period will increase only two days for every additional five years of continuous employment.

In the formula above replace the '6' with the appropriate number of days—this applies to both part-time and full-time employees, including housekeepers and gardeners.

Aguinaldo (Christmas payment)

Aguinaldo is considered a regular part of an employee's wages. It is not a bonus and is required by law to be paid to all employees, full-time and part-time. Payment is to be made before December 20, although many pay a week or more earlier. The Aguinaldo amount to be paid is what an employee would earn over a 15-day period which is half of a typical month

Working on statutory holidays

If an employee is required to work on one of the official government holidays, they receive regular payment for the day plus double time for hours worked. Just to be clear, that adds up to triple time. The days are:

- **January 1:** Año Nuevo (New Year's Day)
- **First Monday of February:** Día de la Constitución (Constitution Day)*

- **Third Monday of March:** Natalicio de Benito Juárez (Benito Juárez's birthday)*
- **May 1:** Día del Trabajo (Labor Day)
- **September 16:** Día de la Independencia (Independence Day)
- **Third Monday of November:** Día de la Revolución (Revolution Day)*
- **December 1:** Transmisión del Poder Ejecutivo Federal (Change of Federal Government)**
- **December 25:** Navidad (Christmas Day)

*These dates vary to tie in with the weekend
**Election years only

Termination pay

Mexican labor laws are pro-worker. This is why employment contracts are so important identifying hours, days of work, duties, expectations and more. Please do consider an employee contract. If you ever have to fire them, it will save you. Sonia Diaz processes many of these contracts and her contact info can be found throughout this book.

Unless termination is voluntary, or justified as per the list below, termination pay includes three months' salary, plus 20 days for each year worked, plus prorated vacation and Christmas pay.

Termination pay must be paid at the time of termination or regular salary shall continue until the termination is paid in full. For example, when there is a labor lawsuit and the employee wins, you not only owe termination pay but salary up until the payment.

If an employee quits voluntarily, termination pay is not required.

Grounds for dismissal

Employees in Mexico can only be dismissed if there is a cause for the dismissal (Article 47, Federal Labor Law). Document any of these instances, and have the employee sign the notes. Causes for dismissal include:

- Use of false documentation to secure employment (this cause applies only within the first 30 days of service)
- Dishonest or violent behavior on the job
- Dishonest or violent behavior against co-workers that disrupts work discipline
- Threatening, insulting or abusing the employer or his or her family, unless provoked or acting in self-defense
- Intentionally damaging the employer's property
- Negligently causing serious damage to the employer's property
- Carelessly threatening the workplace safety
- Immoral behavior in the workplace
- Disclosure of trade secrets or confidential information
- More than three unjustified absences in a 30-day period
- Disobeying the employer without justification
- Failure to follow safety procedures
- Reporting to work under the influence of alcohol or non-prescription drugs
- Prison sentence that makes it impossible for the employee to render the services he or she was supposed to render
- The commission of any other acts of similar severity

The notice of dismissal must be delivered to the employee at the moment of dismissal, setting out the precise causes by which the employee is being terminated.

Procedural requirements for dismissal

Under the Federal Labor Law (FLL), the employer must give the employee notice in writing of the ground for dismissal, or the Labor Board must issue a termination notice which must comply with specific requirements. For example, it must include a detailed description of the facts, dates, times and manner in which the employee incurred the grounds for dismissal. If the notice is presented directly to the employee, two witnesses must be present.

The employer must dismiss the employee within 30 days from the date of the employee's misconduct or from the date the employer became aware of it.

If the employee refuses to accept the notice of dismissal, the employer has five days to file it with the Labor Board. Failure to follow this procedure will presume a wrongful dismissal, and the employee will be entitled to full severance payments.

Reduction in work conditions to the detriment of the employee

The terms and conditions of employment cannot be modified to the detriment of employees, including reduced hours. Unilateral changes that are detrimental to employees can trigger constructive termination of the employment agreement, which requires payment of the full legal severance pay.

Any agreement that causes material damage to the employee's total compensation will be deemed null and void, as employment rights and acquired benefits cannot be waived (ie you can't contract your way out of the law). Any change that leads to a material damage will be null, even where the employee expressly consented to it. If you want to change the working conditions in this manner, you will have to close out the existing contract, pay the termination fees, and begin a new one. It's not easy being an employer in Mexico, especially if your staff is full time.

Working hours and overtime

The working week must not exceed:

- 48 hours a week for day shifts
- 42 hours a week for night shifts
- 45 hours a week for mixed shifts

The working week consists of six working days. However, the daily or weekly distribution of hours can be agreed so that employees have all, or part of, Saturday and Sunday as regular days off.

Employees required to work on Sundays (as a regular work day) are entitled to 1.25% of their usual daily wage for Sunday.

An employee can only be required to work overtime in exceptional circumstances. They are paid double for the first nine hours of overtime per week and triple for any subsequent hours.

Rest breaks

Employees are entitled to at least one full day of rest after six days of work. If employees agree to work on their day off, they receive triple their wages for that day.

In addition, employees are entitled to a rest break of at least 30 minutes during a working day. If the rest break given to an employee is less than 30 minutes long or the employee is not entitled to leave the work facilities to rest, then that rest break must be determined as time actually worked and remunerated.

Sick leave

Employees must obtain a certificate from the IMSS in the case of illness or injury (FLL and Social Security Law of 1997). And this is all part and parcel of why you should be happy to pay IMSS for your employees.

Once a certificate has been obtained from the IMSS the entitlement to sick leave varies—depending on the type of illness and degree of incapacity. The IMSS decides whether sick leave is to be granted, as well as the amount to be paid to employees during the illness or injury. The IMSS pays this amount directly to the employees.

Having full time help is a serious responsibility in Mexico but it's extremely luxurious to be able to have that kind of assistance. Maids and gardeners are a huge plus to this lifestyle. Many of the expats who arrive in Mexico are great employers and wind up treating their staff like family, helping with expensive items and schooling for their children. And such treatment is rewarded with years of loyalty and service.

Chapter 16:

Currencies, banking and taxes

Most of Mexico uses the Mexican peso exclusively. And it is the legal currency. But in gringo areas, many real estate transactions—sales and rentals—are priced in US dollars. Pricing in US dollars itself is not illegal. But, legally, the purchaser can pay the equivalent in pesos according to the current exchange rate.

In places like Puerto Vallarta, San Miguel, Ajijic—anywhere with gringo populations—you'll find many houses are priced in US dollars.

For Canadians and Europeans, it is nasty to have things priced in US dollars when you don't earn US dollars. And when you're in Mexico. In fact, it feels downright presumptuous of them. But in some places, there is nothing you can do about it. The

Americans price this way so they don't have to play any currency games and I get it. Still, there are houses in gringo areas that are priced in pesos—by Mexican owners. You just have to look for them. Often, they are the better deal.

You'll end up playing a currency game when you purchase a home in any foreign currency—with both your capital gains assessment and the final value of your home if you are repatriating the funds. Welcome to the world of Forex.

You're playing a currency game when you buy a house in any foreign country and sell it later. Let me give you an example of an unfriendly exchange rate swing.

Let's say you're American. You found a house you liked for MX$4 million. And bought it in 2008. At the time, the USD rate was MX$10 to US$1. You needed to exchange US$400,000 to make this purchase in Mexico.

Now, years later, you sell the house, which you have renovated, and it is worth MX$8 million—its value has doubled. But does that translate into US$800,000? Not on your life. The rate is now MX$20 per US$1—so it's still worth US$400,000.

But, on the other end of the stick, if you bought an MX$8 million house today for US$400,000, and if the exchange rate went back to 10 to 1 by the time you sold, you'd have doubled your money on the currency game alone. And if the house value increases at the same time, you'll make a killing. But, honestly, there are better ways to participate in this sector of the economy (multiple currencies). It's just something you need to be very aware of when making a major purchase in a foreign currency—you're playing two games, real estate and foreign exchange.

If you're American, it makes sense to buy a house priced and paid for in US dollars. But then, if you're Canadian, British, European, Australian—anything but American—there is no way to avoid this currency game, whether the house is priced in pesos or US dollars. If that's the case, go for the houses priced in pesos, if you can—they are the much better deals.

If your pension or online work pays in another currency while you live in Mexico and you spend pesos on daily living costs—you're always happy to see your currency increase in value, as you get more day-to-day value. But it will wreak havoc on capital investments (such as a house) that have been purchased in pesos, should you intend to repatriate those funds.

Opening a bank account

You'll need copies of your immigration card (or cards, if a joint account) and passports, plus some utility bills proving your address. It takes a very long time and there are multiple forms to sign. I mean hours of sitting around and signing. But you'll find the account very useful. We pay some bills online but have found others more difficult to manage online. However, we keep trying, in the spirit of things always getting better. While Mexico is very advanced on communications, their online systems are often complex beyond necessity. This includes banking and utility websites.

Another thing you will find is that, while you can use your non-Mexican credit cards in Mexico with no problem, there are many utilities such as power and telephone that cannot run a recurring monthly payment on a foreign credit card. Don't ask me why, I have no idea. As a workaround, we instruct them to run an annual amount. There will be many small things like this that can end up irritating you. Just remember, you're in a foreign country. This is not the US or Canada.

Many people in Mexico still pay their bills in cash at a supermarket, convenience store or bank. In fact, although it's changing, Mexico is still a very cash-driven economy and you'll find that many services—even doctors and dentists—require cash payments. And, of course, you pay your maid and gardener cash, unless you make other arrangements with them.

You can also transfer from your bank account to another Mexican account or debit card with online banking. Or deposit cash into someone's account or on their debit card in person at the bank.

Day-to-day things, like paying bills, can take considerably longer in Mexico. Especially if you need to pay cash at a store instead of online from your home. It's all part of living in Mexico and you'll have to get used to it, because it's the way it is.

Foreign money transfers

We have used foreign exchange services to transfer large (house-buying) amounts as they have the best exchange rates. But with fees, that doesn't make sense for the amounts you'll need to transfer for monthly bills or other necessities in Mexico.

We have had great success with TransferWise and there are other services available that are easily found online. Most take less than 48 hours to arrive and can be transferred in cash from your bank account or charged on a credit card.

Home country tax requirements

- **USA:** You will need to declare all worldwide income to the IRS every year and file a tax return no matter what your resident status, unless you renounce citizenship.

- **Canada:** You will remain a Canadian resident for tax purposes unless you jump through the hoops and become a non-resident Canadian citizen. Speak to your Canadian accountant if this is what you would like to do. Among other prerequisites, you will usually be required to close all of your bank accounts and credit cards in Canada. If you own property in Canada, it is a good idea to sell it, if this is the road you wish to travel. Many choose to remain Canadian residents for tax purposes—particularly if their income comes from Canadian pensions and investments. Speak to a tax accountant or lawyer about your options.

- **European Union:** There are no overall rules that dictate how EU expats or people who work and spend time outside their own countries can be taxed. However, it's possible (likely) that the country where you are resident for tax purposes can tax your worldwide income. Please consult an accountant in your home country for details.

Chapter 17:

Buying a home in Mexico

Deed versus fideicomiso

Some property falls within a 'restricted zone' and cannot be owned outright by non-citizens. This includes any land situated within 100 km (60 mi) of an international border and any land situated within 50 km (30 mi) of the ocean. In 1993, this was adapted so that foreigners can purchase property in the restricted zone, but in a trust, with the bank as the holder of the title. It was a way to allow foreign development in tourist zones. This vehicle, or trust instrument, is called a fideicomiso—it remains valid for 50 years and is renewable. It's in your name, but the bank holds the paperwork on your behalf in a trust.

Deed ownership is the type of ownership we are most used to north of the border. There is a title to the land which is held directly by the owner. If you're not in a restricted zone (most of the country), this is the ownership you'll have.

Using an agent

You're going to need a good real estate agent. Everything is different here. You cannot do it alone (at least not the first time—and even the second or third, I wouldn't).

Trouble is, it's hard to tell the good guys from the bad guys. There are no real estate licenses, although some states have started to register real estate professionals. There is no actual multiple listing service (MLS). Although Vivanuncios (www.vivanuncios.com.mx) and Metros Cúbicos (www.metroscubicos.com) can give you some idea. They aren't perfect yet, but they're good for looking around.

If you Google the region you are interested in, you'll come up with dozens of English-speaking real estate brokerages. Sometimes it's better to go with a known name—Century 21, Sotheby's, RE/MAX, Keller Williams Realty and many more are all in Mexico. But remember, these are just franchises. And there is no recourse in this country for a bad real estate agent. None.

Visit a few local real estate websites and send emails. See who is responsive. See who you click with. Ask for recommendations on expat forums and expat Facebook pages.

The big trouble in Mexico is that it's hard to get some agents to point out houses that belong to other brokerages. So, you need to be proactive. Get on *all* the local sites and you tell them which houses you would like to see—and take advice on other houses as well.

The other thing that's trouble is no MLS means no formal market comparison on sales prices. Someone could list a property for $800,000 but only get $500,000—you don't know in Mexico. No formal record. It's all what the agent tells you.

There are good agents out there. But you have to use your gut and find the right one for you.

The buying process

Unlike north of the border, the seller is often in the house and they are at the notario's office with you on both occasions—the signing of the official contract to purchase (our equivalent of an accepted offer) and the closing.

You pay the owner directly in many cases—and that's certainly the case if they are Mexican. On occasion, however, in gringo communities with agencies conducting business in only US funds, there will be a trust account in the US. It actually annoyed me to no end, as a Canadian, to have to transact a real estate deal in New York when I was in Mexico, but you soon learn to shrug your shoulders. It is what it is—this is the US real estate agents' doing.

The deposit is an agreed-upon figure—10% is not uncommon.

And there's an interesting twist. Say I buy a house for MX$10 million. I give the owner a MX$1 million deposit—this transaction takes place in the notario's office at the official signing of the contract to purchase.

Should I, the buyer, default after this, the MX$1 million is the property of the owner. That's like it is in Canada or the US. But, if the owner now decided that he/she doesn't want to sell after all, or defaults in any way, this is where it gets interesting. The owner then gives the buyer's MX$1 million back, plus an additional MX$1 million.

You come to the table with cash (a check will do, but you know what I mean). It's very difficult (if not impossible) to arrange any kind of a mortgage and, if you ever could, it would be at double the rates you are used to paying. Your best bet is to leverage property you already own up north and obtain a line of credit with which to pay cash in Mexico.

Generally, people don't use home inspectors, except gringos. You can find them. You'd generally be given a day or two to inspect the house before signing on the dotted line.

A few months after the transaction is complete, the notario will call to tell you that your deed is ready.

Closing costs

If you're buying a home in Mexico, you will face closing costs of 5–10% of the property's value, including professional fees and taxes. Add 10% in your head to be safe.

> **Ayudita:** Make sure there has been termination of employees before you purchase a home. The employee otherwise goes with the house and, if they have been with the house for some years, are entitled to thousands of dollars in termination pay. See *Chapter 15: Hiring household employees* for details.

Property tax

The property tax on homes (*impuesto predial*) is due January 1 each year, but there are substantial discounts for paying early. Depending on your region and services (cities are generally more expensive) and what you own, your property taxes will range from MX$2,000–8,000 (US$100–400) a year. Kiosks are set up in many cities to facilitate payment, starting in October.

Ayudita: It is *your* responsibility to pay your property tax (and all utility bills). Do not assume that an invoice will arrive in the mail. You need to be proactive and note when bills and taxes are due and make sure you pay them on time.

Ejido land

Usually, ejido land is owned by local communities. They are land grants from the 1910 revolution and are passed from generation to generation within the community. You can buy this land, but it requires agreement from everyone in the community who owns it. You don't always know if the person who is selling this land is actually authorized to do so.

Our advice is to stay away from this kind of deal but, if you absolutely must buy ejido land, insist on a title search and title insurance. It can be expensive, as you often need a legal team to complete the purchase correctly, but it can be done if it's really necessary.

Chapter 18:

Selling a home in Mexico

You're going to need a real estate agent. Real estate agent fees are 6–8% of the selling price but I've paid 10% in San Miguel. You also need to add IVA (16%) onto the agent's commission cost—the seller is responsible for this payment.

Professional fees vary. A good notario will cost you more than a bad one, but they are worth their weight in gold when it comes to figuring out the taxes you will, or won't, owe on your house sale. Pricing varies according to location but could be the equivalent of several thousand dollars. Ask before proceeding and you won't be in for a shock.

If you hold your title inside a fideicomiso—within 100 km (60 mi) of an international border or within 50 km (30 mi) of the ocean—you will also need to budget for the 'trust cancellation fee', which is in the US$1,000 range.

Capital gains exemptions are only available to temporary residents, permanent residents and Mexican citizens. And they aren't really 'capital gains' exemptions as we know them, but more on that later. If you hold a tourist visa or don't otherwise qualify for the (so-called) capital gain exemption, you will pay a 30% flat tax on the gross sale price of your house.

To qualify for capital gains exemption, aside from residency, you must have an RFC (*Registro Federal de Contribuyentes*—a Mexican tax ID number) and you need to attach it to a utility bill for your house. This will prove that you have lived there for the required three years as your principal residence.

The value of the exemption is the peso equivalent of 700,000 UDIs—a national rate which fluctuates and is displayed on the Bank of Mexico (Banxico) website. Currently, it amounts to approximately MX$5.8 million (US$290,000) per person on the title, which can be deducted from the sales price. If two of you are on the title and both qualify, the exemption becomes double (and triple for three, but that's the limit).

You can check the updated value of the UDI on the official Banxico portal.

But there's a catch. This is calculated from the bottom up. For example, if you buy a house and then resell it, they frankly don't care what your purchase price was (unless you are claiming capital renovations with legal facturas—see a notario for details before you start). For the most part, they only care what your selling price is. Let me just do this in one currency to simplify things. If you buy a house, with one person on title and pay US$420,000 and then decide you don't like it and turn around and sell it for the same price, the only portion of that sale price that is *not* taxed is the first US$290,000 (which is currently the exemption allowed by the 700,000 UDIs. I've been told that a good notario can often find some loopholes for you (which is why their services are expensive). Be sure to see one before you purchase to discuss your individual tax liabilities.

The exchange rate might be your friend—or not.

In places like Los Cabos, San Miguel, Ajijic, Cancún and Puerto Vallarta, home prices are often quoted in US dollars. Think about the amount of money you are betting on the exchange rate if you are not American (the cost of a nice house in any of those towns).

The deed will always show the equivalent in Mexican pesos, as will the sales document, even if you price in US dollars.

You're playing a currency game when you buy a house in any foreign country and sell it later.

Suppose you found a house you liked for US$400,000 in San Miguel de Allende. And bought it in 2008. At the time, the US dollar rate was MX$10 to one US$1. The house is recorded as having been purchased at MX$4 million.

Now, years later, you sell the house, which is worth US$600,000. But the record will show MX$12 million (as the rate is now MX$20 per US$1). So, you have a capital gain of MX$8 million—which is US$400,000 equivalent in capital gains to be taxed. But you only actually have US$200,000 profit. Not fun.

Then, if you're Canadian, British or European, add one more currency fluctuation to the risk and mix. You'll have to first purchase US dollars to play this game if the sale is in US dollars. And hope that currency rate is your friend as well.

It can get complicated. You should always know a good notario. Pay for the best. They will guide you.

Capital gains at home

Check with your home country accountant if you are a resident for tax purposes (which many are while maintaining Mexican physical residency). You will likely be subject to capital gains at home on this sale but if you are American or Canadian there is a tax treaty that can provide relief if you have been subject to a capital gains tax payment in Mexico.

Time frames

This is Mexico, so really, you just have to take a few deep breaths and wait. It might sell in a month or two, it might sell in a year. Do everything you can to promote the sale yourself. Make sure that you put the listing on Craigslist (they're all over Mexico) and any other site you can find. Be sure to add it (where allowed) to any gringo groups on Facebook or email groups. And chill. Have a margarita while you're waiting. It will happen.

Chapter 19:

Spanish for expats

Do you have to learn the language? Let's rephrase that. Do you want to assimilate into Mexico and live in a Mexican community or do you plan to stay ensconced in a gringo enclave where everyone speaks English? The location you choose is a large part of your answer.

Most tourist locations on the beach—from Cabo to Cancún—are English-friendly. Ditto gringo-heavy areas like San Miguel de Allende and Ajijic on Lake Chapala. It makes sense—if there are a lot of expats living there, you will find the things that expats are used to, from groceries to restaurant menus to the spoken word.

An interesting observation—I was in the Costco in Cabo San Lucas prior to Easter one year. There were two long rows in the candy/snacks section devoted to Easter eggs and chocolate bunnies and such. Probably 30–35 items.

Cuernavaca, a city getting up toward the million mark, just south of Mexico City, has proportionately fewer gringos (well under 2,000).

And clearly, fewer Easter candy choices. Our Costco had four items.

Easter, you see, is different here. It's called Semana Santa (Holy Week) and, as the name suggests, it lasts for a week. There are incredible fiestas and religious ceremonies—not to be missed. But if you want a more traditional gringo 'Easter', you need to be in a gringo community—or somewhere large, like Mexico City.

But this is about Spanish—and whether or not you need to learn it. It's harder to learn a new language the older you are, that's a fact. But it's good to keep your mind active. Doing nothing in Mexico has its pitfalls—more on that later.

At least learn *some* Spanish. It will save you money in the grocery store. It will help you in restaurants (otherwise you'll be pointing at plates going by to order your meal). If you plan to drive, it would be nice to be able to speak in even limited Spanish if you are pulled over. Our son-in-law once told the police at a traffic stop that he had his 'son in the shrimp'.

Mexico is like everywhere—when newcomers try to learn the language, people are friendly to them because they are trying. It really isn't important that you're perfect. It's important that you try. Even without lessons, you can pick up a few key phrases. Watch Mexican TV. Listen to Mexican radio in the background. It will sink in, slowly.

In larger cities like Guadalajara and Mexico City, many residents are bilingual (or better). But Spanish is the national language and is the default language of the country.

In the smaller towns, even those with a high proportion of gringos, you will not find service people who speak much English. Stores and restaurants, yes. Anyone who makes money catering to gringos, yes. But government services, such as immigration, will be conducted in Spanish.

Don't let that scare you, however. If you just want to come to Mexico and retire and play golf and lie on the beach and not worry about learning Spanish, there are many communities that will be happy to accommodate you. And there are facilitators and translators for hire in every town. It is possible. It all depends on two things—your own desires and the location you choose.

There are many ways to learn Spanish, once you decide to try. I highly recommend a foundation course by Michel Thomas—available free for your smartphone at the App Store, or go to www.michelthomas.com to learn how to purchase courses from iTunes and Amazon. By the time you are done, you'll have a great base from which to continue lessons. Another good choice is Qroo Paul's Spanish lessons which is free online—just Google the title—or get more information in *Chapter 24: Handy guides*.

Then, find a reputable school. If there's not one locally, consider taking three weeks' instruction or more—and consider living with a Spanish family for the duration (immersion Spanish, it's the quickest and most efficient).

Google and TripAdvisor are your friends when it comes to choosing a Spanish school. Most Spanish language schools also offer the immersion method.

If traveling isn't an option for you, consider Skype or Zoom lessons. There are also books, if that is your preferred way of learning—and locals who will work one-on-one with you to teach you the language.

And talk to people. That's the best way. Use your limited vocabulary to learn more.

Chapter 20:

A gringo primer on food in Mexico

Do you know the difference between a taco and a tostada? Between a huarache and a sope? A gordita and a flauta? Pull up a seat and we'll tell you about some of the bases you'll find for Mexican antojitos—literally translated as 'little cravings'. I liken them to tapas and you can find them all over Mexico from street food to fine dining.

We often buy freshly-made bases at the supermarket when company is coming (most larger supermarkets will have an in-store tortilleria)—add a little shredded chicken or pork, some shredded cheese, and pop them in the oven (or toaster oven). Set out little bowls of toppings—chopped lettuce, salsa, sour cream—and you'll have people eating out of their own hands.

The bases

- **Tortillas:** There are yellow corn, blue corn or wheat tortillas available in Mexico. Corn is favored in the south, while wheat is more popular in the north but there's a lot of cross-pollination across the country.

- **Chalupas:** Chalupa means 'canoe'. These are little canoe shaped boats—made of masa flour and deep fried and filled with pork, chicken or beans, and accented with grated cheese, salsa and lettuce.

- **Tostadas:** The word literally means 'toasted' and it's a crunchy, flat, corn tortilla that is used as a base for chicken, pork, seafood or beans with cheese.

- **Gorditas:** These are masa flour pastries, stuffed with meats or cheese. It can be baked or fried—think of it as the Mexican calzone.

- **Huaraches:** These are oblong shapes of fried masa with pinched sides that resemble the popular huaraches sandals of Mexico. They can be filled with chicken, pork or beans—assume everything is topped with cheese.

- **Sopes:** A small circle of fried masa with pinched sides (like huaraches, only circles), sopes are usually filled with black beans and cheese. They are finger food and meant to be eaten in the hand (like tacos and many Mexican antojitos).

Common dishes you may not recognize

- **Carnitas:** Pork marinated with spices, simmered in pork fat and commonly eaten in tacos. It literally means 'little meats'. The process takes 3–4 hours and produces a very rich meat.

- **Chapulines:** These are popular in the area around Mexico City and in Oaxaca and are fried grasshoppers. Commonly eaten in tacos. With *lots* of guacamole in my case. This is seasonal.

- **Escamoles:** Edible ant larvae, harvested from the root of the agave cactus. The same one that makes tequila. Seasonal, and expensive, Mexicans consider this a supreme delicacy. But honestly? To me, it didn't taste like much at all.

- **Chilaquiles:** Served with your choice of red or green sauce and your choice of sunny side up eggs or shredded chicken, chilaquiles are just large corn nacho type chips, simmered in salsa. The green sauce is less hot. It's a breakfast dish.

- **Cochinita pibil:** This is a slow-roasted pork dish from the Yucatán that sees the meat marinated in a very acidic fruit juice and seasoned with annatto seed—giving it a red color. The meat is then roasted in a banana leaf.

- **Masa:** Corn flour (masa harina) or dough for making corn tortillas, tamales and other Mexican foods.

- **Chiles en nogada:** The national dish of Mexico—this is a poblano pepper stuffed with a picadillo, covered in walnut sauce and sprinkled with pomegranate seeds. Red, white and green—viva Mexico. Served everywhere in late August and September but can often be found year-round.

- **Pozole:** Pozole, which means hominy, is a traditional soup or stew made from meat (usually pork) and hominy and garnished with shredded lettuce, thin sliced radishes, chopped onion and lime.

- **Mole:** There are seven kinds of mole, a traditional sauce, but all with one thing in common—chocolate. Both Puebla and Oaxaca states take credit for this culinary wonder—but we'll leave that to them to fight out. As a rule, all mole sauces contain chile, a fruit, a nut, black pepper and chocolate. You can find homemade mole in many of the municipal markets.

- **Menudo:** A Mexican stew/soup made with a red chile base and tripe (beef stomach). Said, in Mexico, to work wonders for hangovers. I wouldn't know (and not because I don't drink).

- **Tamales:** A log shaped chunk of masa dough with filling that is steamed inside a pre-soaked corn husk or, as is the case in the Yucatán, a banana leaf. When made with banana leaves the tamale is flatter and shaped in an erstwhile square. The wrappings on both are discarded before eating. The fillings can vary—everything from meats and cheeses and beans to chocolate. Yes, there are dulce (sweet) tamales—best served warm with whipping cream.

- **Tacos:** A taco can be almost anything as it's simply a corn or wheat tortilla wrapped around a filling. Tacos al Pastor are pork, seasoned with adobada spice before slow roasting on a spit. Tacos de cabeza have to do with various parts of a cow's head and I have no experience to impart. Fish tacos are often fried in batter first and crispy. Shrimp tacos are a staple on the beach. The aforementioned carnitas are a big one, very popular. There's a taco for every taste. And the tacos are usually doubled up, to give a firmer, edible container for the meat. And a quick note—those hard-shell corn tacos? An American concoction—we don't have those here.

A few tips from a gringa

- **Sushi:** Don't do it. They have a lot of sushi places, especially in larger cities or gringo towns. But they put cream cheese in it. And it's not really recognizable if you're a sushi aficionado (but a good try, and my Mexican friends think it's great).

- **Chinese takeout:** It's dicey. I've been looking for a very long time—and having lived a lot of my life between Toronto and Vancouver, I know Chinese food. You might find an okay rendition in a larger city, but trust your instinct. Ask around. Watch where the Chinese eat—and check out who the owners are. Google recipes for your favorite dishes and learn to make them.

- **Turkey:** I also have never been able to approximate the turkey skin that seems to result up north—even though I've bought Kirkland turkeys from Costco. No idea what that's about.

Chapter 21:

Cost of living

Some things are cheaper in Mexico—a lot of things. Anything that involves labor, for one. It's incredible inexpensive to renovate a house. But it takes a long time because they will primarily work by hand.

For us, being Canadian, the price of beer, wine and other alcohol is almost cut in half. But not like that's a good reason to move to Mexico—in fact it is probably one of the dangers. There are some retired expat groups that drink in the bars from 10am–closing, every day. We've seen it in numerous cities—it happens to retirees everywhere around the world. They don't know what to do with themselves—so they drink. Just a caution.

If you are from the US, the difference won't be that stark in booze prices, although imported whiskeys from the US will cost substantially more. If you're from Europe, it will be cheap. It's all perspective, really.

As you have seen in the household employee section, having a housekeeper or gardener is relatively cheap.

Today, I have a housekeeper at US$25 a day (and a full day) but 4 days a month, so that's US$100. Not much difference, really, although it happens more often. And my garden help up north came once a month for US$60. Here, they come every week for about US$120 a month. So, I can't say the help is cheaper, but I do have more of it.

Communications, as you read in *Chapter 12*, are cheap. The same cable, phone and internet package we have here for about US$60 would cost US$150+ at home. And our US$15 cell phone plans cost US$80 each in Canada. So those are savings.

Rents and home costs vary greatly, but utilities such as telephone, internet, electricity, gas, gasoline and water are relatively consistent. And if one shops at local markets or farmers' markets, items such as clothes, fruits, vegetables, chicken, beef, pork and housewares are very inexpensive. Every town and city has these markets, some permanent and some two or three days a week. They are often referred to as tianguis.

The produce at smaller markets, *tianguis*, and local stands—as well as at small butchers and bakeries—is incredible and very inexpensive. That said, it takes time to go to these markets and buy chicken from one vendor, pork from another, broccoli from one, mangoes from another, and on and on. And you need to make sure you have small bills for when you go.

If you go to the supermercados like Superama, La Comer, Fresko and Mega, you will probably pay double for the produce. And you'll pay more for the meat (but not double). But you can put it all in one basket and check out with a credit or debit card. For me, often the time factor has me shopping in supermarkets. Where things are still incredibly inexpensive. But the best value and freshest food is at the local markets, no question. And imported items you buy in Costco will cost more than they cost at home.

We had been paying US$1,200 a year up north for car insurance, and that was reduced to US$400. But our health insurance, which we don't pay for in Canada, became more than US$800 a month down here. Things start to even out. Excluding our pre-existing conditions. That's private medical care, which we have decided to drop. See *Chapter 14: Can I get healthcare?* to read more about that.

We recently installed solar panels because with the pool and pond we use a lot of power. Our consumption been in the 'red', which pretty much doubles your bill. Power in Mexico is sold under different tiers—the less you use, the less you pay per kWh. Once you hit the red tier, the highest level, you must maintain the lowest level in use for six months before your bill is adjusted again.

So, while it can be inexpensive if you don't use much power, if you're a power-hungry house, it can get expensive. Our power bills for two months were topping MX$15,000 (US$750). You need to judge your requirements and act accordingly. We have pumps, a pool and pond, extra coolers and, while our dryer is gas, it still uses power. We have lots of company and all use computers and TVs—but our lights are all LED.

Our gas use is relatively cheap and works out to about MX$700 (US$35) a month. Automobile fuel will seem expensive if you are from the US, cheap if you are from Canada or Europe.

That said, if you don't drive and if you shop at the markets, you can live here pretty cheaply. I know of people who rent small, perfectly acceptable houses and live happily on US$1,500 in pensions per month. Of course, the more money you have, the more things you can do, but a lot of people do move to Mexico because their money goes further.

Tipping in Mexico

Tipping is frequent in Mexico, but in small amounts. Always try to keep your pockets full of change and small bills. Small bills are a good idea in smaller stores anyway—they have a hard time making change. We've made a list for you of customary tipping situations and the appropriate amounts.

Many of these positions, such as grocery store baggers and parking lot attendants are not paid and their tips are the only income they earn. You will hear on some gringo forums or groups that it's not good to tip too much. We call bullshit. These people can really use the money, they work hard for their tips and you can afford it. What's MX$20 (US$1) to you? It means a kilo (2.2 lb) of beans and a large bag of rice for them.

- **Cab drivers:** We will tip MX$10–20, depending on the fare. Which is so inexpensive.

- **Gas station attendants:** We round up. When spending MX$500 on gas, we ask for MX$480 and tip them MX$20. In percentages, 3–5% works.

- **Grocery store baggers:** I had a Mexican friend chastise me for always tipping at least MX$10, even when it's only a bag or two. Seriously? What's MX$10 to me? Even being Canadian, that's about 65¢. If I have 10 bags, I usually give them MX$20.

- **Porters (at the airport and bus station):** I give them MX$50, as I usually have two heavy bags. But MX$10 a bag is adequate.

- **Restaurant staff:** The usual 10–20%, depending on service, is normal.

- **Restroom attendants:** MX$10 is an acceptable tip.

- **Stoplight performers:** You'll see (in the cities at least) people performing at stoplights, sometimes juggling, sometimes unicycling, sometimes eating fire! Tipping is at your discretion. I do like to give these guys MX$20, because no one else ever does (I'm told they get a peso or two—5–10¢).

- **Windshield washers:** You can wave them off, but if you use them (and most of them do a great job)—MX$10–20 is normal. These are primarily found in cities.

Chapter 22:

Cost of dying

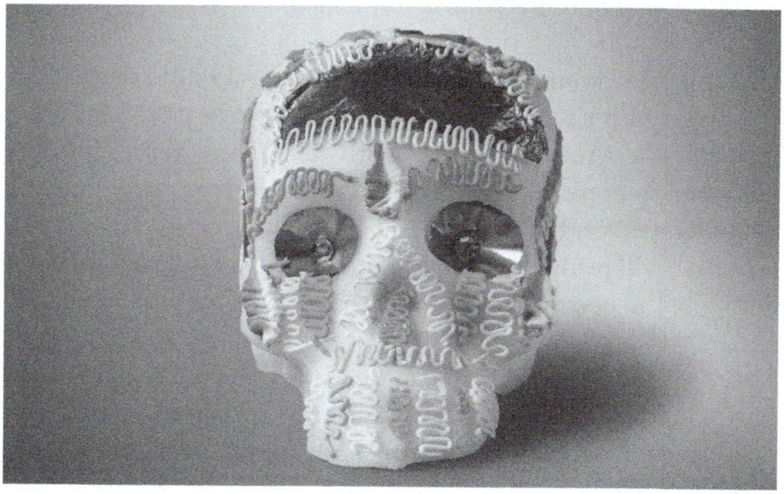

Death and estate planning

Like living in Mexico, dying in Mexico has financial advantages. Recent examples of cremation costs, including pick up of the body and delivery of the urn, average about MX$10,000 (US$500). But first you need to get through the paperwork. Or, more accurately, your representative does.

Mexican authorities require identification documents both for the deceased and for the family member or representative collecting the body. Your representative should be prepared to provide the necessary passports, birth certificates and marriage certificates.

Some funeral homes, especially those in large expat communities, offer programs where you can prepay funeral services.

Mexican funeral homes will expect payment in advance and your representative should be prepared to cover these costs if you have not already done so. If you wish to be returned home for burial, it could cost up to US$10,000 to repatriate your remains (unless you are cremated first in Mexico).

Death in Mexico normally requires a funeral home representative to go with a family representative to the *Registro Civil* (civil registry office) to register the death. The family representative will need to present identification for both themselves and the deceased person (passports are best). The funeral home representative will bring the required documents pertaining to when and how the person died.

The Registro Civil will issue a death certificate. It is very important at that time to ask for additional certified copies of the death certificate, typically five or more copies. Keep the original in a safe place.

If the deceased had resident status you must inform the INM (Instituto Nacional de Migración). If the deceased was married, you also need to inform INM of the change in marital status of the spouse to widow or widower. You must present both the visa and birth certificate of the deceased. If the person had permission to work, SAT (the tax office) must also must be notified. There are no other Mexican requirements.

Your executor should contact the local embassy in Mexico for precise instructions on dealing with the death of a loved one in Mexico.

- **Americans:** For the death of an American in Mexico, the Special Consular Services (SCS) unit of the US Citizen Services section at the US embassy can assist family and friends in the event of the death of a US citizen in Mexico. Contact the US embassy for further information.

- **Canadians:** The death of a Canadian in Mexico requires a family representative to go to the Canadian Embassy. This person must have their Canadian passport and birth certificate. Power of attorney is required if you are not immediate family and is recommended under any circumstances. They must also have the passport belonging to the deceased person as well as the original or a certified copy of the death certificate.

Mexican wills

If you own property or have any Mexican holdings, including a bank account, do yourself a favor and get a Mexican will. Well, do your heirs a favor, I guess, technically. While ultimately you may be able to prove that a Canadian or US will is valid, it will take years. In September, wills are drawn up at half price, nationwide. It's like national will month.

And it's different again than drawing up a will back home. It will take some time to create a will, including several appointments. An official translator will be involved unless you are fluent in Spanish, as well as three personal witnesses you bring with you. There are a lot of details that aren't required up north. And it's a very impressive looking document—almost as impressive as your deed.

When you open a bank account, you must designate a beneficiary. And when you buy property within a fideicomiso (bank trust for waterfront or border property), you designate a beneficiary. However, a will is still an integral part of this process. By now, you know how much they like paperwork and stamped paperwork here in Mexico.

To change the title or ownership of a property or to settle an estate in Mexico, you should contact a local lawyer or notario.

Chapter 23:

Action plan for your move

Before your move

Do your research. Narrow down the places that you think you'd like to live. Visit them. For at least a month at a time if you can. Once you know where, you can start the process.

Have you got your appointment at the Mexican consulate yet? Got all that paperwork together? The first order of business is to get that holograph in your passport.

Identify a facilitator to walk you through the immigration process once you arrive in Mexico—you're not done, not by a long shot.

Figure out how you're going to transfer funds on a regular basis—a visit to your bank to chat with a manager is in order. Some banks have simple options in place, some don't. Do register with online services—such as TransferWise—ahead of time so you've got a leg up by the time you get there. Are you keeping your credit cards? Any bills you'll have coming—be sure to switch them to electronic delivery.

If you're driving, have you arranged for Mexican car insurance? Are you familiar with the TIP (temporary import permit) process for your vehicle?

Are you sending your goods with a mover? If so, do you have your ducks in a row?

If you're moving pets, make sure you have all their documentation—health certificate, rabies/distemper certificate and parasite-free certificate.

Do you have all the prescription medicine you will need until you get settled? Don't forget—bring them in their original bottles and if you have any psychotropics or antibiotics, make sure you have your original prescription.

What are you doing for health insurance once you arrive?

Cleaning out your home

Make three piles and be ruthless:

- Thrift store/garage sale
- To put in storage (if you are doing that)
- To take to Mexico

Less is more. You can buy most things you need in Mexico. And if you're looking to buy a home in a gringo town, many are sold fully furnished, down to linens and dishes. And furnished rentals are widely available. Another plus in gringo towns is resale shops for furniture and decor.

During your move

If you've double-checked everything and you're good to go, then relax and enjoy the trip. Whether you are flying or driving, make sure that Migración (Mexican immigration) checks the 'canje' box on your white form. We can't say this enough. Also, if you're driving, don't drive at night in Mexico. And make sure you have enough cash (pesos) for the toll roads to get you where you are going.

After your move

Head to Migración immediately to begin processing your pre-approval for your resident visa. The visa you have now is only good for 30 days following your entry to Mexico. Do not delay.

Make a Mexican will.

Learn to speak Spanish (if you haven't already).

If you drive, get a Mexican driver's license. You don't have to give up your current license (but it won't be valid unless you keep it current).

If you drove to Mexico, remember that your car and your TIP are attached to your visa—which is only for 30 days. You will need to notify Aduana (customs) when you receive your new resident visa and have them attach the vehicle to your new file.

Please see www.SoniaDiazMexico.com for further info.

Chapter 24:

Handy guides

Making phone calls

Calling emergency services anywhere in Mexico
- Dial 911

Calling USA or Canada from Mexico (all included in your monthly Telmex bill, as well as many European locations)
- 001 + *[area code]* + *[7-digit number]*

Calling Mexico from USA or Canada
- 011 + 52 + *[area code]* + *[7- or 8-digit number]*—011 is international code, 52 is the country code for Mexico, area codes are 3-digits, numbers are 7 digits (8 digits in Mexico City)

Calling toll-free numbers in the US and Canada from Mexico— use this chart to substitute the number in the right-hand column

USA/Canada toll-free	In Mexico dial
1-800	001-880
1-844	001-885
1-855	001-884
1-866	001-883
1-877	001-882
1-888	001-881

Common acronyms

Abbreviations in Spanish are quite confusing to gringos. This is a small list of some that are used quite often (in alphabetical order).

- **CDMX:** Ciudad de Mexico (Mexico City). Until a few years ago, it was known as DF (Distrito Federal).
- **CFE:** Comisión Federal de Electricidad (the power company). There's only one. It's run by the feds.
- **CURP:** Clave Única de Registro de Población. Essentially a social security number needed to enroll in healthcare, schools, and other governmental procedures.
- **FMM:** Forma Migratoria Múltiple. Used to keep track of everyone entering and exiting the country who does not hold a Mexican passport.
- **IMSS:** Instituto Mexicano del Seguro Social—provides health, pension and social security services.
- **INAPAM:** Instituto Nacional de las Personas Adultas Mayores. Senior citizen agency (including issuing discount cards).
- **INM:** Instituto Nacional de Migración. The immigration agency of the Mexican government.

- **IVA:** Impuesto al Valor Agregado. The national sales tax, which is currently 16%.
- **MXN:** Mexican peso. The official currency of Mexico.
- **NUE:** Número Único de Extranjero. Directly translated as unique foreigner number. Every foreigner with a residency visa has a NUE.
- **NUT:** Número Único de Trámite. A number to identify procedures at the federal government level—for example, anything to do with the residency visa process.
- **PROFECO:** Procuraduría Federal del Consumidor. Mexico's consumer protection agency.
- **RFC:** Registro Federal de Contribuyentes. A Mexican tax ID.
- **RP:** Residente Permanente. Permanent resident visa. Enables you to reside in Mexico indefinitely.
- **RT:** Residente Temporal. Temporary resident visa. Enables you to reside in Mexico for up to four years.
- **SAT:** Servicio de Administración Tributaria. The agency responsible for all matters related to federal tax collection.
- **TIP:** Temporary Import Permit. Required to import a foreign-plated vehicle, motorcycle or RV.

Major fiesta days in Mexico

* Civic holiday (observed, but employees not entitled to a day off)

** Statutory holiday (employees entitled to a day off)

January 1
Año Nuevo (New Year's Day)**

This national holiday is the quietest day in Mexico. Businesses are closed and most people stay home or attend church.

Ayudita: Happy New Year is *Feliz Año Nuevo* in Spanish. If you don't understand what the tilde (~) does to the pronunciation, you might just avoid the phrase for now. Ano, without the tilde, means asshole (and you'll feel like one).

January 6
Día de los Reyes Magos (Epiphany/Day of the Three Kings)

This day commemorates the three wise men presenting gifts to baby Jesus. In the past, this was the day that the Mexican kids got their presents, not Christmas Day. And they didn't hang stockings, they left their shoes outside the door for the kings to fill with goodies. There's been a lot of US influence, primarily though television, but also with the arrival of swaths of expats over the years. Now Christmas Eve, in most locations, is the larger celebration with a few gifts reserved for January 6.

And there is always the *rosca de reyes*, a very special cake. A small clay doll is baked inside the cake for Epiphany—and whomever gets the figurine must host a tamale party on February 2. The baby Jesus is symbolic of hiding Jesus during Herod's Massacre of the Innocents. There is a whole lot of Jesus symbolism going on in this country, as you will soon see.

February 2
Día de la Candelaria (Candlemas)

This is a blessing of the candles ceremony that marks the end of winter. But more importantly, it's the tamale party—hosted by the person who found the baby Jesus in their cake on January 6.

First Monday of February
Día de la Constitución (Constitution Day)**

This national holiday honors the 1917 Mexican constitution—the result of the revolutionary war of 1910.

Third Monday of March
Natalicio de Benito Juárez (Benito Juárez's Birthday)**

This national holiday celebrates one of Mexico's most beloved presidents.

Easter Celebrations—dates vary

Carnaval takes place at assorted locations across Mexico the three days preceding Ash Wednesday and the beginning of Lent. In many markets across Mexico, you'll find vendors selling cascarónes prior to this date—hollowed egg shells filled with confetti. Children will meet in the main square during the Carnaval days and smash the eggs on each other's heads.

- Maundy Thursday*
- Good Friday*
- Holy Saturday**
- Easter Sunday**

Semana Santa (Holy Week)—dates vary

There are somber processions carrying the crucified body of Jesus and lighthearted gatherings to blow up paper mâché Judas figures (created to resemble modern-day politicians). There are Chichimeca dancers replete in feather and seashell anklets, dancing up a storm in the squares. Businesses close during this week of Mexican national vacations. Reservations to anywhere are often made a year in advance—many Mexican families go on vacation together this week. Often, expats prefer to hunker down and enjoy local festivities.

May 1
Día del Trabajo (Labor Day)**

This is a large national holiday—workers hold parades and everything is closed.

May 5
Cinco de Mayo (Fifth of May)*

While this is national observance, it's primarily celebrated in Puebla—commemorating the defeat of the French at the Battle of Puebla. In America, you'd think this was the biggest holiday in Mexico (Cinco de Mayo). Not so. You won't even notice it in most of the country.

September 16
Día de la Independencia (Independence Day)**

One of the biggest in Mexico, this celebrates Mexico's independence from Spain with parades, picnics, and parties. Lots of red, white and green.

At 11pm on September 15, the president gives the famous *Grito* (the 'cry'—Viva Mexico!) from the National Palace in Mexico City. It is a spectacular, over-the-top event in the nation's capital. El Grito is repeated in numerous town squares across the country, but with particular vigor in the colonial highlands—Dolores Hidalgo, San Miguel de Allende, Guanajuato and Querétaro, which are known as Mexico's cradle of independence. The schedule of events is exactly the same in every village, town and city across Mexico.

November 1/2
Día de Muertos (Day of the Dead)*

This national observance spans two days, beginning at midnight on October 31. *Día de Todos los Santos* (All Saints' Day) on November 1 honors deceased children and *Día de los Fieles Difuntos* (All Souls' Day) on November 2 honors deceased adults. Born out of the clash between Aztec ritual and Spanish colonialism more than 500 years ago, this important Mexican celebration contains elements of both Paganism and Christianity. Conjuring up dead ancestors, cooking favorite foods to serve at their graves and creating elaborate private shrines, decorated with dancing skeletal figures, is all just part of this magnificent cultural event.

While the food and specifics will vary from area to area, it is without a doubt one of the most important fiestas in Mexico. And almost all families will begin the holiday with a trip to the cemetery on October 31 at midnight, bringing toys for the children and tequila for the adults (yes, the dead ones). The ornate sugar skulls made for the children are truly works of art.

In some areas it is customary to spend the night—where bells are rung for the spirits every 30 seconds, from midnight until dawn, to 'wake' the dead. Gravestones are cleaned and decorated. It's a huge family reunion, both dead and alive, with hibachis and cooking, drinking, guitar-playing with storytelling—and memories shared by the lights of hundreds of candles.

It is the way that the legends and lore of ancestors stay alive from generation to generation. Sometimes even mariachi bands play. But above all, it is a time for reuniting with those who have transcended this lifetime.

One of the most famous celebrations takes place on the island of Janitzio in Lake Pátzcuaro. Boats are decorated with candles and flowers and taken to the island's cemetery, where they spend the night summoning the dead.

Third Monday in November
Día de la Revolución (Revolution Day)**

Commemorates the start of the Mexican Revolution in 1910, which ended the struggle against then-dictator (and president) José de la Cruz Porfirio Díaz Mori.

December 12
Día de la Virgen de Guadalupe (Day of the Virgin of Guadalupe)

The party begins at the crack of midnight on the Virgin of Guadalupe's birthday, when all the mariachis in the town square begin playing *Las Mañanitas, The Birthday Song*. And then you've got continuous parties, fireworks, dancing, rodeos, parades and street fairs.

The Virgin of Guadalupe is largely responsible for the indigenous Mexicans finally accepting the Catholicism that the Spanish foisted on them. When the apparition of a Mexican Virgin Mary appeared to the peasant Juan Diego on a hill outside Mexico City in December of 1531, it changed everything. And a staggering number of miracles, interventions and cures are attributed to her as 10 million people visit her basilica (on that same hill) every year. Hers is the most visited Catholic church in the world, next to the Vatican. Quite the lady.

December 16–24
Las Posadas (Christmas Posadas)

For nine nights before Christmas, locals don costumes and re-enact the pilgrimage by Joseph and Mary, and their search for a room. Door-to-door candlelit processions pass through various colonias, hosted by churches, businesses and community organizations. The last house is the where that night's fiesta is held, complete with a piñata.

December 25
Navidad (Christmas)**

Mexicans often consider the Christmas season to begin on December 12, on the Virgin of Guadalupe's birthday, returning to work after New Year's Day. Many businesses close (including Migración) and reopen on January 7, after Epiphany.

December 31
Año Nuevo (New Year's Eve)

New Year's Eve in Mexico is typically spent with family. According to Mexican custom, you should eat 12 grapes at midnight and make a wish for each grape, toss 12 coins in front of your door and sweep them in for financial luck, and take your suitcase for a walk to ensure upcoming travel in the new year.

In addition, there are many regional celebrations, from gourmet food events, to sailfish tournaments, to silver fairs, to hot air balloon festivals.

Every town has local saints and celebrations, some more than others. In tourist towns, you'll have a lot more noise, especially in the town centers—fireworks and *cohetes* (bottle rockets). It's a (some think not so) charming tradition left over from the Aztecs. On fiesta days, they set off bottle rockets before dawn to wake up the sun. In San Miguel one morning, from 4:30–5:30am, we calculated 20,000 bursts. As they say, check your local listings for events near you.

Help with your Spanish—common words and phrases

These are just a few words to get you started. You need to study Spanish!

Common phrases

Good morning	Buenos días
Good afternoon	Buenas tardes
Good evening/night	Buenas noches
Hello	Hola
How are you?	¿Cómo estás?/¿Qué tal?

What's happening?	¿Qué tal?
Fine thank you, and you?	¿Bien, gracias y usted?
Where is the bathroom?	¿Dónde esta el baño?
Can you help me, please?	¿Puedes ayudarme por favor?
Do you speak English?	¿Usted habla inglés?
I don't speak Spanish	No hablo español
How much does it cost?	¿Cuanto cuesta?
It doesn't work	No funciona
Do you take credit cards?	¿Aceptan tarjetas de crédito?
See you later	Hasta luego
Goodbye	Adiós
Excuse me (with permission)	Con permiso
Don't worry about it	No se preocupe
Do you have change?	¿Usted tiene cambio?
Please/Thank you	Por favor/Gracias

In grocery stores—basic food and drink

apple	manzana
avocado	aguacate
bacon	tocino
beans	frijoles
beef	res
beer	cerveza
blueberries	moras azules
bread	pan
butter	mantequilla
cake	pastel
cheese	queso
chicken	pollo
coffee	café
cookies	galletas
corn	maíz
cranberries	arándanos
eggs	huevos
fish	pescado
flour	trigo
fresh	fresco
fruit	frutas

garlic	ajo
ice (bag)	hielo (bolsa)
ice cream	helado
juice (apple, orange etc)	jugo (de manzana, naranja etc)
lettuce	lechuga
meat	carne
milk	leche
oil	aceite
onion	cebolla
oranges	naranjas
organic	orgánico (remember your cognates)
pork	cerdo
potatoes	papas
raspberries	frambuesas
rice	arroz
shrimp	camarones
sour cream	crema acidificada
strawberries	fresas
sweets	dulces
sugar	azúcar
tea, black	té, negro
tea, green	té, verde
tomatoes	jitomates
vegetables	vegetales
water	agua
whipping cream	crema para batir
whole wheat	integral
wine (red)	vino tinto
wine (white)	vino blanco

Ayudita: Eggs are not refrigerated in Mexico. They will keep a month or so. Canada and the US are the only countries I know of that refrigerate eggs and it has to do with washing the protective layer off the shell.

False friends

We have what are called false friends in Spanish—words that sound so similar to an English word, that you are sure they are the same. But not so. Some can be downright embarrassing. Like *embarazada*, for example.

Spanish word	You think it means	It really means
asistir	assist	attend
balde	bald	bucket
basamento	basement	base of column
bigote	bigot	mustache
bizarro	bizarre	noble, brave
delito	delight	crime
despertar	desperate	to wake up
destituyo	destitute	fired
embarazada	embarrassed	pregnant
enviar	envy	to send
éxito	exit	success
fabrica	fabric	factory
largo	large	long
molestar	molest	to annoy
once	once	eleven
pie	pie	foot
preservativo	preservative	condom
rapista	rapist	barber
recordar	record	to remember
ropa	rope	clothing
sano	sane	healthy
sopa	soap	soup

These are but a few examples, please feel free to Google 'false friends Spanish' for a more comprehensive list.

But have no fear—cognates are here

And now that we've told you this, let us also tell you that you already know thousands of words in Spanish if you speak English. Seriously. Or as they say in Spanish, *verdad* (truth)!

They're called cognates. Egad, we hadn't planned to give you a Spanish lesson, but this is important for building confidence. You know more than you think you do. We'll give you some examples and let you Google the full list (Google *Spanish English words that are the same*).

Some words are identical but pronounced differently—we'll be leaving the pronunciation to the teachers. These are some of the 'perfect' cognates—we have just given you the words that start with A, B, and some of the Cs—you can already see how many there will be.

English	Spanish	English	Spanish
actor	actor	carton	cartón
admirable	admirable	central	central
agenda	agenda	cerebral	cerebral
alcohol	alcohol	chocolate	chocolate
altar	altar	circular	circular
animal	animal	civil	civil
area	área	club	club
artificial	artificial	collar	collar
auto	auto	colonial	colonial
balance	balance	coma	coma
bar	bar	combustion	combustión
base	base	conclusion	conclusión
brutal	brutal	conductor	conductor
cable	cable	confusion	confusión
canal	canal	considerable	considerable
cancer	cáncer	control	control
cannon	cañón	cordial	cordial
capital	capital	criminal	criminal

We're not nearly done. We meant it when we said thousands of words.

Here's another cognate that is nearly the same in both languages. And as above, we will give you a few examples of each cognate, but please Google the full list of Spanish/English cognates.

Here is a simple rule for nouns ending 'tion' in English—replace the 'tion' with a 'ción'.

English	Spanish	English	Spanish
accusation	acusación	celebration	celebración
admiration	admiración	combination	combinación
association	asociación	condition	condición
attention	atención	constitution	constitución

Wait, there's more.

English nouns ending 'ary' are converted to Spanish by replacing the ending with 'ario'.

English	Spanish	English	Spanish
adversary	adversario	glossary	glosario
anniversary	aniversario	primary	primario
arbitrary	arbitrario	salary	salario
commentary	comentario	solitary	solitario

English adjectives ending 'ic' can be converted to Spanish by replacing with a 'ico'.

English	Spanish	English	Spanish
academic	académico	basic	básico
alcoholic	alcohólico	classic	clásico
artistic	artístico	democratic	democrático
automatic	automático	domestic	doméstico

English adjectives ending 'ous', replaced with a 'oso'.

English	Spanish	English	Spanish
curious	curioso	numerous	numeroso
delicious	delicioso	precious	precioso
glorious	glorioso	religious	religioso
mysterious	misterioso	tedious	tedioso

Nouns ending 'ct', replaced with a 'cto'.

English	Spanish	English	Spanish
abstract	abstracto	correct	correcto
act	acto	exact	exacto
compact	compacto	perfect	perfecto
conflict	conflicto	product	producto

There, now don't you feel better already? Don't forget to Google the full lists!

Ayudita: In most cases (there are exceptions) Spanish does not double up on letters ('attention' becomes 'atención' and 'glossary' becomes 'glosario').

Mexican slang and swearing

And because it always makes you feel better, here's a little Spanish slang and a few swear words:

A huevo	Hell, yeah
A la verga	OMG
Chela	Cold one (beer or drink)
Chido	Cool (as in hip)
Chocolas	Gimme five
Cojones (or huevos)	Balls
Crudo	Hungover
Fresa	Yes, strawberry, but also a snob

Güey (pronounced 'wey')	Guy, mate, bud, dude, you get it—if someone calls you 'wey', it's a good thing
Jeta	Resting bitch face
Me vale madre	I don't give a f**k
Naco	Tacky
¡No mames!	WTF!
¡No manches!	No way!
¡Órale!	Go for it, let's do it, onward!
Pinche	No direct translation (pronounced 'pinchay') but it kind of means 'f**king'—as in pinche gringo
Pendejo	Technically, it means pubic hair but is used as a slang for idiot, imbecile, moron and so on
¿Que onda?	What's up?
Vales verga	You are a useless dick

Online shopping (in your pajamas)

- **Amazon (www.amazon.com.mx):** Safe, secure and they've got most everything. And, you can sign on using your Amazon account from your own country.

- **Amazon USA (www.amazon.com):** If you can't find it on the Mexican Amazon site, there are many US sellers who will ship to Mexico and the prices aren't that bad.

- **Apple (www.apple.com.mx):** If you've got a Mac, iPad, iPhone or Apple Watch, you'll want to bookmark this one.

- **Borderfree (www.borderfree.com):** Delivers to Mexico from hundreds of US stores with no fuss, no muss, no bother.

- **Costco (www.costco.com.mx):** Doesn't have everything the stores have and has limited food and drink but we bought our commercial stove there—there are also a lot of items that are not available in store. And they deliver—bonus for heavy items.

- **Crate and Barrel (www.crateandbarrel.com.mx):** Expensive, but they're expensive north of the border, too.

- **Hierbas Orgánicas (www.hierbasorganicas.com.mx):** Great spot to get all the hard-to-find herbs and spices—and as a bonus, they're organic!

- **Home Depot (www.homedepot.com.mx):** Regular old Home Depot online—fast delivery.

- **Mercado Libre (www.mercadolibre.com.mx):** Great place to shop for everything from dog food to furniture—and a secure payment system. You don't even have to use a credit card if you don't want to—you can pay cash for your purchase at any Oxxo with Mercado Pay.

- **Sephora (www.sephora.com.mx):** What can we say—it's Sephora online.

Supermarkets that deliver

- **Chedraui (www.chedraui.com.mx)**
- **La Comer (www.lacomer.com.mx):** Includes La Comer, Fresko and City Market
- **Superama (www.superama.com.mx)**

All things legal

- **Sonia Diaz (www.SoniaDiazMexico.com):** Sonia Diaz, Facilitator for visas and more (across Mexico)

Spanish language

- **Spanish Vocabulary (www.spanishvocabulary.ca):** A fantastic resource of Spanish words by category

- **Qroo Paul (www.qroo.us):** See *Spanish Lessons* tab
- **Michel Thomas Method (www.michelthomas.com)**

Real estate

While not quite as efficient as the multiple listing service (MLS) in Canada and the USA, these sites can give you a good idea of properties available for sale or rent across Mexico and what you will need to budget.

- **Metros Cúbicos (www.metroscubicos.com)**
- **Vivanuncios (www.vivanuncios.com.mx)**
- **MercadoLibre (inmuebles.mercadolibre.com.mx)**

You can also search for rentals online:

- **Locanto (www.locanto.com.mx)**
- **Mitula (www.mitula.mx)**

Prescription drug names—USA, Canada and Mexico

USA	Canada	Mexico
Accupril	Accupril	Acupril
Achromycin	Achromycin	Acromicina
Aciphex	Pariet	Pariet
Actonel	Actonel	Actonel
Actos	Actos	Zactos
Adalat	Adalat XL	Noviken LP
Adderall	Adderall	-
Advair	Advair	Seretide
Aldactone	Aldactone	Vivator
Allegra	Allegra	Alegra
Allegra D 12 hour	D-Allegra	Allegra-D
Alphagan P	Alphagan	Aggla Ofteno
Altace	Altace	Tritace

USA	Canada	Mexico
Amaryl	Amaryl	Diaglim
Ambien	Stilnoct	Nocte
Amoxil	Amoxicillin	Acimox
Antivert	Bonamine	Bonadoxina
Astelin	Astelin	Amsler
Atacand	Atacand	Bloresss
Atarax	Atarax	Atarax
Ativan	Ativan	Ativan
Augmentin	Augmentin	Acimox AC
Avalide	Avalide	Coaprovel
Avandia	Avandia	Avandia
Avapro	Avapro	Aprovel
Bactrim	Sulfatrim DS	Soltrim
Bactroban	Bactroba	Sinepbac
Benicar	Benicar	Almetec
Benicar HCT	Benicar HCT	-
Bentyl	Bentyol	Bentil
Benzaclin	Benzaclin	Benzaclin
Biaxin XL	Biaxin	Adel
Buspar	Buspar	Buspar
Calan	Isoptin	Dilacoran
Capoten	Capoten	Brucap
Cardura	Cardura	Cardura
Cartia	Cartia	Angiotrofin
Catapres	Catapres	Catapresan
Ceftin	Ceftin	Cefabiot
Cefzil	Cefzil	-
Celebrex	Celebrex	Celebrex
Celexa	Celexa	Citox
Cialis	Cialis	Cialis
Cipro	Cipro	Bacprocin
Clarinex	Aerius	Aviant
Cleocin	Dalacin-C	Biodaclin
Cogentin	Cogentin	-
Colchicine	Colchicine	Colchiquim
Combivent	Combivent	Combivent
Concerta	Concerta	Concerta
Cordarone	Cordarone	Braxan

USA	Canada	Mexico
Coreg	Coreg	Dilatrend
Cortef	Cortef	Efficort
Coumadin	Coumadin	Coumadin
Covera	Veralan	Cronovera SR
Cozaar	Cozaar	Cozaar
Crestor	Crestor	Crestor
Cymbalta	Cymbalta	Cymbalta
Darcocet	-	Neo-Percodan
Deltasone	Deltasone	Ednapron
Depakote	Divalproex	Epival
Desyrel	Desyrel	-
Detrol LA	Detrol LA	Detrusitol
Diflucan	Fluconazole	Alumet
Digitek	Lanoxin	Lanoxin
Dilantin	Dilantin	Epamin
Diovan	Diovan	Diovan
Diovan HCT	Diovan HCT	Co-Diovan
Ditropan	Ditropan	Inprax
Dor	Cosopt	Trovost
Duragesic	Duragesic	Durogesic
Effexor XR	Effexor XR	Benolaxe
Elavil	Amitriptyline	Anapsique
Elidel	Elidel	Elidel
Eskalith	Eskalith	Carbolit
Estrace	Estrace	Armistor
Evista	Evista	Evista
Fioricet	Novogesic	-
Flexeril	Flexeril	Yuredol
Flomax	Flomax	Asoflon
Flonase	Flonase	Flixonase
Flovent HFA	Flovent HFA	Flixotide Nebs
Folic Acid	Folic Acid	Valdecasas AF
Fortamet	Metformin	Aglumet
Fosamax	Fosamax	Blindafe
Glucophage	Metformin	Aglumet
Glucotrol	Glipizide	Flumedil
Glucotrol XL	Glucotrol XL	Minodiab
Glucovance	-	Bi-Pradia

USA	Canada	Mexico
Humalog	Humalog INS	Insulin Lispro
Humulin 70-30	Humulin 30-70	Humulin 70-30
Humulin N	Humulin N	Humanilusin
Hycotuss	-	-
Hydrodiuril	HCTZ, HCT	Acortiz
Hytrin	Hytrin	Adecur
Hyzaar	Hyzaar	Hyzaar
Imitrex	Imitrex	Fermig
Inderal	Inderal	Inderalici
Indocin	Indocid	Antalgin
Keflex	Cephalexin	Ceporex
Kenalog	Triaderm Top	-
Klonopin	Clonazepam	Clonapilep
Klor-Con	K-Dur	Corpotasin LP
Lamictal	Lamictal	Lambdra 12 24
Lamisil	Lamisil	Binafex
Lantus	Insulin Lantusa	Lantus
Lasix	Semide	Lasix
Lescol	Lescol	Lescol
Levaquin	Levaquin	Cina
Levitra	Levitra	Levitra
Levoxyl	Synthroid	Tiroidine
Levsin	Pro-Banthine	-
Lexapro	Lexapro	Lexapro
Lidex	Lyderm	Topsyn
Lidoderm	Lidoderm	-
Lioresal	Baclofen	-
Lipitor	Lipitor	Lipitor
Lodine	Ultradol	-
Lomotil	Lomotil	Lomotil
Lopid	Gemfibrozil	Raypid
Lopressor	Metoprolol-L	Mezelol
Lotensin	Lotensin	Lotensin
Lotrel	Lotrel	-
Lotrisone	Lotriderm	Gelmicin
Lunesta	Lunesta	-
Macrobid	Macrobid	Furadantina
Maxzide	Triazide	-

USA	Canada	Mexico
Medrol Oral	Medrol	-
Methadose	Methadone	-
Mevacor	Mevocor	Dilucid
Micronase	Glyburide	Brucen
Minocin	Dynacin	Micromycin
Mobic	Mobicox	Aflamid
Monopril	Monopril	-
Morphine	Morphine	Analfin
Motrin	Ibuprofen	Actron
Mycostatin	Nystatin	Micostatina
Namenda	Namenda	Akatinol
Naprosyn	Naproxen	Bruproxen
Nasacort AQ	Nasacort AQ	Nasacort AQ
Nasonex	Nasonex	Elovent
Neurontin	Gabapentin	Bapex
Nexium	Nexium	Nexium
Niaspan	Niaspan	Hipocol
Nitroquick	Nitrostat	Nitradisc
Nolvadex	Nolvadex	Bagotam
Norvasc	Norvasc	Avistar
Novolog	Novorapid	Novorapid
Omnicef	Omnicef	Omnicef
Oxycontin	Oxycontin	Oxycontin
Pamelor	Aventyl	-
Patanol	Patanol	Patanol Al
Paxil	Paxil	Aropax
Paxil CR	Paxil CR	Xerenex
Penicillin VK	Pen Vee K	Anapenil
Pepcid	Pepcid	Androtin
Peridex	Peridex	-
Phenergan	Panectyl	-
Phenergan Cod	Phenergan Cod	-
Phenergan DM	Phenergan DM	-
Phenobarbital	Phenobarbital	Alepsal
Plaquenil	Plaquenil	Plaquenil
Plavix	Plavix	Iscover
Pravachol	Pravastatin	Astin
Prelone	Prednisolone	Fisopred

USA	Canada	Mexico
Premarin	Premarin	Elrredin
Prempro	Premplus	Premelle
Prevacid	Prevacid	Imidex
Prinivil	Lisinopril	Alfaken
Prometrium	Prometrium	Gepromi
Proscar	Proscar	Borealis
Protonix	Pantoloc	Ciproton
Provera	Methiopropamine (MPA)	Megestron
Prozac	Prozac	Farmaxetina
Pulmicort	Pulmicort	Entocort
Pyridium	Phenazo	Pirimir
Quinine	Quinine	-
Reglan	Metoclopramide	Carnotprim
Relafen	Relafen	Nalflam
Remeron	Remeron	Comenter
Restoril	Restoril	-
Rheumatrex	Rheumatrex	Dermox
Rhinocort AQ	Rhinocort AQ	Aerosial
Risperdal	Risperadal	Norispez
Seroquel	Seroquel	Seroquel
Sinemet	Sinemet	Cloisone
Sinequan	Sinequan	Sinequan
Singulair	Singulair	Singulair
Skelaxin	Skelaxin	-
Soma	Soma	Somacid
Spiriva	Spiriva	Spiriva
Strattera	Strattera	Strattera
Synthroid	Levothyroxine	Levhexal
Tamiflu	Tamiflu	Tamiflu
Tegretol	Tegretol	Brucarcer
Tenoretic	Tenoretic	Tenoretic
Tessalon	Tessalon	Capsicof
Thyroid, Armour	Thyroid	-
Tobradex	Tobradex	Tobracort
Topamax	Topamax	Topamax
Toprol-XL	Lopressor SR	Lopresor-R
Tussionex	Tussionex	Tussionex

USA	Canada	Mexico
Tylenol Cod	Tylenol Cod	Tempra CD
Ultracet	Ultracet	Tramacet
Ultram	Ultram	Citra
Valium	Diazepam	Ifa Fonal
Vasotec	Vasotec	Ileveran
Ventolin Inhaler	Salvent	Salbutalan
Viagra	Viagra	Patrex
Vibramycin	Vibramycin	Vibramicina
Vicodin	Vicodin	-
Vigamox	Vigamox	Vigamoxi
Vistaril	Hydroxyzine Pamoate	-
Voltaren	Voltaren	Artrenac
Wellbutrin Sr	Wellbutrin	Butrew 12-24
Xalatan	Xalatan	Gaap Ofteno
Xanax	Alprazolam	Alzam
Xopenex	Xopenex	-
Zantac	Ranitidine	Acloral
Zestoretic	Zestoretic	Zestoretic
Zetia	Ezetrol	Zient
Ziac	Monocor	Biconcor
Zithromax	Zithromax	Amsati
Zocor	Zocor	Colesken
Zoloft	Zoloft	Aleval
Zovirax	Zovirax	Rapivir
Zyloprim	Allopruinol	Atisuril
Zyprexa	Zyprexa	Zyprexa
Zyrtec Tab	Reactine Tab	Cetitev
Zyrtec-D	Reactine-D	Cetitev-D

Epilogue

We've come to the end of our journey—and the beginning of yours.

We've given you the knowledge you will need to start your adventure—now the ball is in your court.

We can almost guarantee that you'll have more questions and we're happy to help any way we can—you can get in touch on Sonia's website or visit us on Facebook and we'll try to help.

And because things change in Mexico, and change often, we hope you'll visit www.SoniaDiazMexico.com regularly for news, or follow her on Facebook at www.facebook.com/SoniaDiazMexico.

Just who are the authors and what qualifies them?

Sonia Diaz has been consulting on immigration and relocation projects in Mexico for more than a decade and has processed thousands of applications and other submissions for services and permits. She has offices in San Miguel de Allende and Puerto Vallarta with services available in all of Mexico. She runs the highly popular website, www.SoniaDiazMexico.com with helpful information for those who wish to come to Mexico. Her intent is to inform, to be concise and accurate. A Mexican national, all of Sonia's information is based on extensive experience and her English is impeccable. Sonia offers a range of consulting services designed to help you make your life in Mexico easier.

A Canadian expat and affirmed wanderer, Beverley Wood is a producer, consultant and author who has explored and written about popular locations in Mexico since 2003. After living in assorted states and cities in Mexico, she settled on Cuernavaca as her Mexican base, 50 miles south of Mexico City. Having gone through the immigration process herself, and having wandered through much of Mexico, she has lots of first-person advice (and opinions) to share. She also consults on relocation to both Mexico and Canada for select clients (beverleywood@gmail.com).

A note from Sonia

Each day my husband and I say how grateful we are for the support of our clients. I have a career I love. And I have a fantastic team working with me, including those not so obvious.

I was raised in Mexico City by amazing parents. My parents, four siblings, a niece and I lived in a 50 square meter (550 square foot) apartment with two bedrooms, one very small bathroom and bunk beds. My two brothers and mother still live there. My father, who recently died at age 95, worked mostly as a waiter. it is amazing how we even managed. But we have a supportive, loving family.

Shortly after I graduated in human resources, I lived in many places in Mexico, returning to Mexico City for several years and raising a daughter on my own for her first three years. It was not easy, and I say this so others realize I am very well aware of how difficult it is for some. We all have our stories and our history.

Fourteen years ago, I met my Canadian husband and taught myself English. After a year in Ajijic, we tried Canada—in the winter. Brrrrr! I have also visited the US several times. All these experiences have given me a better perspective of life in the rest of North America.

We came to San Miguel 13 years ago. We rented two different homes and then we bought an extremely basic house with a mortgage. It was fun and educational doing improvements and learning about construction, remodeling and landscaping in this climate.

Again, I write this noting how humble our beginnings were in SMA. We take nothing for granted and we know the benefits of hard work, treating others with respect and treating them professionally.

—Sonia Diaz, San Miguel de Allende, Mexico

Made in United States
North Haven, CT
25 May 2025

69009520R00147